PENSIONS:
REFORM, PROTECTION AND
HEALTH INSURANCE

LEO A. FELTON
EDITOR

Novinka Books
New York

Copyright © 2006 by Novinka Books
An imprint of Nova Science Publishers, Inc.

All rights reserved. No part of this book may be reproduced, stored in a retrieval system or transmitted in any form or by any means: electronic, electrostatic, magnetic, tape, mechanical photocopying, recording or otherwise without the written permission of the Publisher.

For permission to use material from this book please contact us:
Telephone 631-231-7269; Fax 631-231-8175
Web Site: http://www.novapublishers.com

NOTICE TO THE READER

The Publisher has taken reasonable care in the preparation of this book, but makes no expressed or implied warranty of any kind and assumes no responsibility for any errors or omissions. No liability is assumed for incidental or consequential damages in connection with or arising out of information contained in this book. The Publisher shall not be liable for any special, consequential, or exemplary damages resulting, in whole or in part, from the readers' use of, or reliance upon, this material.

This publication is designed to provide accurate and authoritative information with regard to the subject matter covered herein. It is sold with the clear understanding that the Publisher is not engaged in rendering legal or any other professional services. If legal or any other expert assistance is required, the services of a competent person should be sought. FROM A DECLARATION OF PARTICIPANTS JOINTLY ADOPTED BY A COMMITTEE OF THE AMERICAN BAR ASSOCIATION AND A COMMITTEE OF PUBLISHERS.

Library of Congress Cataloging-in-Publication Data:
Available Upon Request

ISBN: 1-59454-704-1

BLACKBURN COLLEGE
LIBRARY

Acc No. BB49176

Class No. UCL 331.2522

Date 4\11\2011

Published by Nova Science Publishers, Inc. ✦ New York

CONTENTS

PREFACE

Older Americans are a powerful force in America politics because of high participation in elections and active lobbying organizations. In addition, the younger set who pay the largest taxes keep a steady eye on the often shifty actions of politicians with regard to pensions. This book deals with some of the critical issues of health insurance for retirees, reform of pensions plans and company actions with regard to pension plans.

In: Pensions: Reform, Protection and Health Insurance ISBN: 1-59454-704-1
Editor: Leo A. Felton, pp. 1-42   © 2006 Nova Science Publishers, Inc.

Chapter 1

DEFINED BENEFIT PENSION REFORM FOR SINGLE-EMPLOYER PLANS[*]

Neela K. Ranade and Paul J. Graney

SUMMARY

There is considerable interest this year in reform of the laws governing funding of single-employer defined benefit pension plans and premium structure for the Pension Benefit Guaranty Corporation (PBGC). Large and growing deficits for the PBGC and continued underfunding of pension plans, particularly for financially weak companies, are the major reasons behind the push for reform.

This chapter outlines the complex current law governing the funding of single-employer defined benefit pension plans. It discusses the role of the PBGC in insuring pension benefits, the structure of the premiums that single-employer plans must pay the PBGC, and the benefits guaranteed by the PBGC in exchange for the payment of premiums. The chapter also describes reporting and disclosure requirements that apply to plans.

The Administration, early in 2005, proposed comprehensive reform of pension funding rules, PBGC premium structure, and reporting and disclosure requirements. Under the proposed approach, the interest rates used for pension funding would be based on a yield curve of corporate bond

---

[*] Excerpted from CRS Report RL32991. Updated July 14, 2005.

rates. This chapter describes the Administration proposal and provides a simple example to illustrate calculation of a liability using a yield curve.

Elements of the Administration proposal form the basis of some of the bills that have been introduced in the 109th Congress. Other bills emphasize features not included in the Administration proposal. Several bills have been introduced in the 109th Congress including H.R. 2830 (the Pension Protection Act of 2005), S. 219, (the National Employee Savings and Trust Equity Guarantee Act of 2005), and H.R. 1960 and H.R. 1961 (each titled the Pension Preservation and Savings Expansion Act of 2005). Other bills include H.R. 2233, S. 991, H.R. 2327, S. 1158, S. 685, H.R. 2106, and S. 861.

This chapter includes quantitative analysis based on regulatory filings by pension plans for 2001 and 2002 to provide an assessment of the number of plans that might be affected by certain elements of the Administration proposal. It also summarizes the reaction to the Administration proposal by business and labor.

The chapter also includes an illustration of the effect on a hypothetical plan sponsor's plan contribution and funded ratio of the credit balance approach used in current law versus the Administration proposal.

The PBGC also insures multiemployer pension plans. The laws and issues relating to multiemployer plans are quite different than for single-employer plans. This chapter focuses on single-employer plans.

Winnie Sun, actuarial intern in the Domestic Social Policy Division, contributed analysis of Form 5500 Schedule B data.

BACKGROUND

The Pension Benefit Guaranty Corporation (PBGC) is the federal agency that insures most defined benefit pension plans. The PBGC posted a deficit (excess of its liabilities over assets) of $23.3 billion as of September 30, 2004.[1] While the PBGC has sufficient assets to pay benefits for the interim future, without changes in the law governing PBGC premiums and funding of pension plans, it is estimated that the PBGC will run out of cash within the next 20 years.[2] The PBGC deficit has created alarm and raised the specter of an eventual taxpayer bailout of the PBGC. In May 2005, a federal bankruptcy court approved the termination of United Airlines' underfunded pension plans which will result in the largest loss to date in PBGC's history. Several other airlines are financially weak and have severely underfunded pension plans that may be terminated.

Since the passage of the Omnibus Budget Reconciliation Act of 1987 (OBRA-87) and until 2003, the interest rate used to calculate *current liability* that is used to determine pension plan contributions was based on the rate on 30-year Treasury bonds. When the Treasury stopped issuing 30-year Treasury bonds in September 2001, it was necessary to provide an alternative. The *Pension Funding Equity Act of 2004*, P.L. 108-218, provided a temporary solution for years 2004 and 2005 by requiring that the interest rate be based on the rate on high quality long-term corporate bonds. This provision expires at the end of 2005 and without action by Congress, the interest rate will revert to that based on long-term Treasury bonds.

In the 30 years since the passage of the *Employee Retirement Income Security Act (ERISA)* in 1974, pension law has become increasingly complex with a patchwork of legislation passed to meet the immediate and varying needs and interests of different parties. In a departure from the incremental pension reform approach used in the past, the Administration early in 2005 proposed fundamental reform of pension funding rules, the PBGC premium structure, and reporting and disclosure.

Several bills are currently under consideration. Some build on the Administration proposal while others introduce elements not seen in the Administration proposal. H.R. 2830 was ordered to be reported by the House Education and Workforce Committee on June 30, 2005, and is currently under consideration by the House Ways and Means Committee.

CURRENT LAW [3]

Overview

By law, plan sponsors generally must make annual contributions to the pension plan so that plan assets are available to pay pension benefits promised to employees. The defined benefit pension system is currently underfunded. The PBGC estimates that total plan underfunding on a termination liability basis was $450 billion as of September 30, 2004.[4] Although plan sponsors are required to make contributions to pension plans, the law provides so many exceptions and overrides that even a sponsor of a substantially underfunded pension plan can go several years without making any contributions to its pension plan.[5] The interest rate used to determine the contribution to a pension plan is another area of focus since the temporary provisions of the Pension Funding Equity Act of 2004 expire at the end of 2005. We provide below an overview of funding rules for single-employer defined benefit pension plans.

When underfunded pension plans terminate, the financial burden is placed on the PBGC which had a deficit of $23.3 billion as of September 30, 2004. The PBGC's large deficit is the result of two factors; substantial underfunding in plans that have terminated in the past, and inadequate levels of premiums paid by plan sponsors to the PBGC. We provide below a description of premiums payable to the PBGC, benefits guaranteed by the PBGC, and the PBGC's (limited) right to assets of sponsors of terminated plans.

Under current law, pension plans are required to file information related to funding and funded status with the Department of Labor (DOL), Internal Revenue Service (IRS), and the PBGC. In addition, summary information must be provided to plan participants. However, restrictions on disclosure of certain information may result in participants being unaware of a plan being severely underfunded until it is on the brink of termination. We provide below an overview of the reporting and disclosure requirements under current law.

Pension Funding Rules

Under current law, the sponsor of a defined benefit pension plan must make a contribution to the plan each year that is at least as large as the minimum required contribution and no larger than the maximum deductible contribution.[6] The original rules relating to minimum required and maximum deductible contributions were laid out by ERISA and were fairly straightforward. These rules allowed the plan's actuary to use one of several acceptable actuarial funding methods[7] and an interest rate based on his/her best estimate of anticipated experience under the plan. The original calculations are now supplemented by calculations based on a comparison between the plan's assets and a more standardized measure of the plan's liability, known as the *Current Liability.*

The current liability is defined as the present value of plan benefits that have accrued as of the valuation date determined with the use of standardized interest and mortality assumptions specified by law. Several other technical terms are used in pension funding law. The common ones are defined in the box on page 4.

There is less flexibility in the choice of the interest rate for determining current liability than for determining the normal cost and accrued liability under the plan's funding method. **Table 7** in **Appendix 1** provides additional information on current liability and accrued liability.

Pension funding terminology
Actuarial funding method — An orderly method of developing the costs of a pension plan such that the payment of these costs will accumulate to the reserve required at retirement age. A plan's funding method determines the normal cost and accrued liability for the plan based on the demographics of plan participants and actuarial assumptions.
Actuarial assumptions — Assumptions that are required to determine the funding calculations. Primary among these are the *interest rate* assumption for the return expected to be earned by plan assets and the *mortality* assumption for the plan participants.
Actuarial present value — The value of future benefit payments discounted with interest to the current time to take into account the time value of money and adjusted to reflect the probability of payment by use of decrements for death, turnover, retirement and disability.
Normal cost — The portion of the actuarial present value of total pension benefits that is attributable to the current year's service under the actuarial funding method chosen for the plan.
Accrued liability — The portion of the actuarial present value of total pension benefits that is associated with the past under the actuarial funding method.
Actuarial Value of plan assets (AV) — Takes into account the fair market value of plan assets (MV) and may smooth fluctuations in MV by gradually recognizing appreciation or depreciation of plan assets over no more than five years. Under current law, the AV must be between 80% and 120% of the MV. The AV is used in the determination of the minimum required and maximum deductible funding limits.
Funding Standard Account (FSA) — An accounting device included in Schedule B of the Form 5500 that the plan sponsor must file each year. It is used to monitor compliance with the minimum funding rules. Charges to the FSA consist of the normal cost and amortization of unfunded liabilities. Plan contributions are credited to the FSA.
Credit balance — The balance created in the Funding Standard Account when the plan sponsor makes a contribution in excess of the minimum required contribution. It is carried over with interest at the rate assumed in the plan's funding calculations and may be used to reduce the employer's plan contribution for the following year.

Historically, the interest rate used to determine current liability was based on the rate on 30-year Treasury bonds. When the Treasury Department stopped issuing 30-year bonds in September 2001, it allowed contributions to be determined based on the rates on existing long-term Treasury bonds for plan years 2002 and 2003.[8] However, with the ceasing of issuance of new 30-year Treasury bonds, the rates on existing 30-year Treasury bonds dropped. Use of a lower interest rate leads to higher pension contributions. The business community would likely have found continued use of a required interest rate based on rates on existing Treasury bonds unfair. In addition, rates on existing long-term Treasury bonds could only serve as a temporary proxy for the rate on 30-year Treasury bonds, given that no new

30-year Treasury bonds have been issued since 2001. It was necessary to find a different solution for the current liability interest rate. The Pension Funding Equity Act (P.L. 108-218) came up with a solution, but only for two years. It specified that for plan years 2004 and 2005, the interest rate for determining the current liability must fall within 90%-100% of the four-year weighted average of rates on long-term corporate bonds.

A term used in the definitions of the minimum required and maximum deductible contributions is the *Full Funding Limitation*. The full funding limitation (FFL) is the excess, if any, of: (1) the accrued liability under the plan (including normal cost); over (2) the lesser of (a) the market value of plan assets or (b) the actuarial value of plan assets. However, the full funding limitation may not be less than the excess, if any, of 90% of the plan's current liability (including the current liability normal cost) over the actuarial value of plan assets.[9]

Minimum Funding Rules

The minimum required contribution is generally equal to the sum of the normal cost and the amortized amount of the unfunded accrued liability (accrued liability less actuarial value of plan assets), reduced by the Funding Standard Account (FSA) credit balance. The FSA is used to track contributions made by a plan sponsor in excess of the minimum required contribution. **Appendix 2** provides a numerical example of a FSA under current law and under possible alternative definitions.

Interest is accrued on charges and credits in the FSA at the rate assumed for determining the plan contribution under the plan's funding method. This rate is chosen by the plan's actuary so that together with other assumptions such as mortality, employee turnover, etc., it represents his best estimate of anticipated experience under the plan.

Additional funding requirements apply to certain underfunded plans. Under special funding rules, called the "deficit reduction contribution" rules, a plan with over 100 participants may be required to make additional funding contributions under certain conditions.[10] The additional funding contribution requirements generally apply when the actuarial value of the plan's assets is less than 90% of the current liability.[11]

Calculation of the additional contribution under the deficit reduction contribution rules is complex and involves a faster amortization of the plan's unfunded liability for a plan that has a low ratio of current liability to the actuarial value of plan assets.[12] The law contains an override provision that specifies that the amount of the additional required contribution may not exceed the amount needed to bring the plan's actuarial value of plan assets to the level of its current liability.

Regardless of whether the deficit reduction contribution rules apply, no contributions are required under the minimum funding rules in excess of the Full Funding Limitation.

Under the Pension Funding Equity Act of 2004, commercial airlines, steel manufacturers, and certain other employers may elect to use special rules to reduce significantly the deficit reduction contribution for plan years beginning between December 28, 2003 and December 27, 2005.[13]

Maximum Deductible Contributions

The maximum deductible contribution determined under the plan's funding method is generally equal to the normal cost plus a 10-year amortization of any unfunded accrued liability. However, the maximum deductible contribution may not be greater than the full funding limitation. Under a special rule, a plan sponsor may deduct amounts contributed to the plan that are not in excess of the amount necessary to bring the plan's assets up to the current liability, without regard to whether the plan assets exceed the accrued liability under the plan's funding method.

Impact of Funding Rules on Funded Status

Three elements of the funding rules have contributed to the underfunding of pension plans in recent years and changes in these have been incorporated in many legislative proposals for funding reform:

- The definition of the Full Funding Limitation is based on 90% of the current liability, not 100% of the current liability. Also, the threshold for triggering of additional contributions under the deficit reduction contribution rules is based on 90% of current liability rather than 100% of current liability.
- The asset measure used in the definitions of the unfunded accrued liability under the plan's funding method, the Full Funding Limitation, and the threshold for triggering of additional contributions under the deficit reduction contribution rules is based on the actuarial value of plan assets. In years of market decline, the actuarial value can be higher than the market value due to the deferral of recognition of capital losses. For such years, the required contributions for plans that choose to spread capital losses (and gains) can be significantly lower than if the market value of assets was used.

- The credit balance in the Funding Standard Account is credited with interest at the assumed interest rate and may be used to lower the required funding contribution even when plan assets have suffered major losses and fallen below plan liabilities.

While the above elements of current funding rules may be appropriate for ongoing healthy plans, they can substantially contribute to the existing underfunding of plans of financially weak companies that are close to termination.

Role of the PBGC

The PBGC was established under ERISA to provide mandatory pension insurance for defined benefit pension plans. The premiums that companies pay for this insurance help to finance the benefits that PBGC distributes to beneficiaries of underfunded terminated plans. The assets taken over from those plans, investment earnings, and any recoveries from sponsors of terminated plans are the other sources of these benefit payments.

PBGC Premiums

The single-employer program has two different premium rates. The annual *flat-rate premium* that every sponsor pays was raised by Congress to $19 per participant in 1991 and has remained unchanged since then. The *variable-rate premium* is charged to certain underfunded plans. It was last modified in 1994 and is currently $9 per $1,000 of the plan's unfunded vested benefits. The plan's unfunded vested benefits are defined as the excess of the plan's current liability, taking into account only vested benefits, over the actuarial value of the plan's assets.[14] However, a plan with unfunded vested benefits is nevertheless exempt from paying variable rate premiums if the plan was at full funding limit for the prior plan year, i.e., the sponsor had made a plan contribution for the prior plan year not less than the Full Funding Limitation for the prior plan year under Section 412(c)(7) of the Internal Revenue Code (IRC).

The interest rate used to determine vested benefits for purposes of calculation of the variable premium differs from the rate used for funding purposes. For plan years 2001 and before, it was 85% of the rate on 30-year Treasury bonds. P.L. 107-47 changed it to 100% of the rate on 30-year Treasury bonds for plan years 2002 and 2003. P.L. 108-218 further modified it to 85% of the rate on long-term corporate bonds for plan years 2004 and

2005. In the absence of new legislation, the rate will revert to the rate based on long-term Treasury bonds. **Table 7** in **Appendix 1** provides additional information on the determination of the present value of vested benefits for purposes of determination of the variable-rate premium.

Guaranteed Benefits

Under ERISA, no further service credit is earned toward accruing benefits, vesting, and entitlement to retirement subsidies once a plan is terminated. As of that date, the plan administrator allocates the plan assets among six priority categories as the statute dictates. If there are not enough assets to pay all the benefits that have accrued, the PBGC takes over the plan as trustee and pays the plan participants guaranteed benefits. Only basic benefits are guaranteed and benefits from new plans and recent amendments are phased in at the rate of 20% per year for five years.[15] Non-vested pension benefits are not guaranteed.

The maximum PBGC guarantee per covered participant is $3,801.14 per month at age 65 for plans terminating in 2005, and is reduced for benefits commencing prior to age 65. This provision has caused considerable distress to retired pilots of airline pension plans terminating with insufficient assets. Under federal regulation, airline pilots are forced to retire at age 60.[16] The maximum PBGC guaranteed benefit for a pilot who retired at age 60 and whose pension plan terminated in 2005 would be $2,470.74 ($3,801.14 times 0.65), considerably lower than the typical pension benefit for a full service airline pilot that might amount to $10,000 per month.

Contingent benefits such as those that have been promised in a case where a plant shuts down are only guaranteed if the precipitating event takes place before the termination date. This is why PBGC will try to terminate a plan before a company triggers shutdown benefits by closing its plants. Since contingent benefits cannot be prefunded, they can place a great strain on PBGC's resources.

Lien Against Plan Sponsor Assets

When a plan sponsor does not make required contributions to the plan, it weakens the plan's funded status and increases the potential claim against the PBGC. Both ERISA and the IRC give the PBGC the right to perfect a lien against the assets of a plan sponsor and members of its controlled group when $1 million in required pension contributions are missed, but only if they have not filed for bankruptcy. The Bankruptcy Code currently keeps the PBGC from perfecting a lien against the debtor, and effectively prevents it from requiring further contributions to the plan.

PBGC's Right to Recovery for Unfunded Benefits

The law allows the PBGC to attempt to recover monies for unfunded pension liabilities from other assets of the plan sponsor. When the PBGC does make recoveries on its claims for unfunded benefit liabilities, it shares the proceeds with beneficiaries who are not receiving the full benefits to which they were entitled under the plan. In the event that sufficient monies are recovered, a plan participant's benefit could be higher than the maximum PBGC guaranteed benefit. ERISA prescribes the use of an average recovery ratio over the five years immediately preceding the year in which the plan terminates instead of using the actual amount recovered for each individual plan. For very large plans with over $20 million in participants' benefits losses, the actual amount of the recovery is used to determine how much will be allocated to the participants. Any amounts recovered from the plan sponsor for contributions that were due before termination are considered as plan assets as of the termination date and are distributed in the same manner as the rest of the assets available at that time. All amounts are determined according to the actual amount recovered for the specific plan regardless of the size of the recovery.

Reporting and Disclosure Requirements

Both ERISA and the IRC require defined benefit plans to provide annual information related to funding and the funded status of the plan to the IRS, DOL, and PBGC. Certain reports and notices must also be provided to participants and beneficiaries on an annual basis. There are additional reporting requirements for underfunded pension plans.

Form 5500

A qualified pension plan generally must submit an annual report (Form 5500) with information pertaining to the qualification, financial condition, and operation of the plan. Form 5500 must be filed with the DOL seven months after the end of the plan year unless the available 2½-month extension has been granted. A defined benefit plan subject to minimum funding standards of ERISA generally must include an actuarial statement on Schedule B that is certified by an actuary enrolled to practice before the IRS, DOL, and PBGC. The Schedule B includes information on the plan's assets, accrued and current liabilities, contributions from the sponsor, expected payments to beneficiaries, actuarial cost method and actuarial assumptions, and amortization bases established during the plan year. The Schedule B also includes the Funding Standard Account statement for the plan year. The DOL forwards a copy of the Form 5500 including the Schedule B to the IRS and the PBGC.

Summary Annual Report

The plan administrator must send a summary of the annual report (SAR) to participants and beneficiaries with basic financial information about the plan. The SAR must state whether or not the contributions to the plan were enough to meet the minimum funding standards and the amount of any deficit. In the case where the plan's assets are valued at less than 70% of the current liability under the plan, the SAR must state the percentage of such current value of the plan's assets. The SAR must be provided within nine months after the end of the plan year or within two months after the extended due date for the Form 5500, if applicable. In addition, upon written request, a plan participant must be provided with a copy of the full annual report (Form 5500).

Participant Notice of Underfunding

Under ERISA Section 4011, plan administrators of certain underfunded plans must notify participants and beneficiaries annually of the plan's funding status and the limits of the PBGC's guarantee. A Participant Notice is due two months after the due date (including extensions) for the Form 5500. The plan administrator of any single-employer plan for which a variable rate premium (VRP) is payable for the plan year is required to issue a Participant Notice, unless the plan meets the *Deficit Reduction Contribution (DRC) Exception Test* for the plan year or the prior plan year. A plan meets the DRC Exception Test for a plan year if the actuarial value of plan assets is at least 90% of the current liability. A plan with actuarial value of plan assets between 80% and 90% of current liability will still meet the DRC Exception Test if the actuarial value of plan assets was at least 90% of current liability in two consecutive years out of the last three years.

Section 4010 Disclosure

Section 4010 of ERISA requires the reporting of plan actuarial and company financial information by employers with plans that have (i) aggregate unfunded vested benefits in excess of $50 million (determined on a variable-rate premium basis), (ii) missed required contributions in excess of $1 million, or (iii) outstanding minimum funding waivers in excess of $1 million. Filing is on a controlled group basis.[17] The information is required to be filed with the PBGC and includes the plan's fair market value of assets and its termination liability. **Table 7** of **Appendix 1** provides additional information on determination of the termination liability for Section 4010 disclosure purposes. Plan sponsors must provide Section 4010 information within 105 days after the end of their "information year." This is April 15 for most employers.

Section 4010(c) prohibits the PBGC from disclosing §4010 information, except for information that is otherwise public. As a result, plan participants of severely underfunded pension plans of financially troubled companies may be unaware of the extent of the problem until the company is in bankruptcy reorganization and the plan is about to be taken over by the PBGC.

ADMINISTRATION PROPOSAL[18]

The Administration proposes a comprehensive overhaul of the laws governing the defined benefit pension system. The proposal included in the FY2006 budget submission consists of a three-pronged approach to reform: changing the rules for funding defined benefit plans, improving the financial position of the PBGC, and improving disclosure to better inform workers, investors, and regulators.

Changing the Funding Rules

In place of the various measures of pension liabilities described above, the Administration proposes the adoption of a single measure of liabilities based on benefits earned to date with minimal smoothing. The proposal would also adjust the funding target of a plan according to the financial strength of the plan sponsor. The time allowed to make up shortfalls would be shortened, and limitations would be placed on benefit enhancements and accelerated distributions during periods of severe underfunding. The final change in funding rules would allow plans to make additional deductible contributions during periods of favorable economic conditions.

Measuring Assets and Liabilities

The Administration's position is that the smoothing available under current law masks the underlying financial weakness of many underfunded pension plans. Its proposal would measure assets at fair market value on the valuation date for the plan (the first day of the plan year for plans with more than 100 participants, or any day of the plan year for smaller plans). For a healthy plan sponsor, the funding target would be based on its *ongoing liability*. The ongoing liability like the current liability is defined as the present value of benefits earned to date. However, the discount rate used to calculate the plan's ongoing liability as of the valuation date would be based on a spot yield curve of high quality corporate bonds. This concept is explained below in the 'Yield Curve Proposal' section. There would be a three-year phase-in period. Projections of future salary increases would not be used in determining the present value of expected benefit payments, but plans would be required to include the likelihood of lump sum payments in calculating their liabilities. The spot yield curve would eventually be used in determining lump sum payments, but this would have a longer phase-in period than its use in determining liabilities and funding requirements.

The proposal would also include additional costs in determining what it calls the *at-risk liability* of a plan that is financially weak. While plans with ongoing liability would rely on relevant recent historical experience in setting assumptions for age at retirement and lump sum elections, at-risk plans would be required to assume that participants would retire at the earliest opportunity and take a lump sum or another form of distribution that results in the largest liability for the plan. A loading factor that reflects the administrative costs of terminating the plan would also be included in at-risk liability.

Funding Targets

The proposal would link a plan's funding target to the financial health of the plan sponsor. The minimum required contributions of a firm with debt that is rated as investment grade would be enough to fund its ongoing liability including the normal cost for the current plan year. A financially weak firm would be responsible for funding its at-risk liability including a loading factor of $700 per participant plus 4% of the at-risk liability. Presuming that the at-risk liability would be significantly higher than the ongoing liability, the proposal provides for a phase-in period of five years during which the actual funding target for financially weak firms would be a weighted average of the ongoing and at-risk targets.

Time Allowed to Make Up Shortfalls

A seven-year amortization period would be established for funding any shortfalls (amounts by which the asset value of a plan is below its funding target on the valuation date). The plan sponsor would be required to amortize the shortfall in level amounts over the next seven years. On the valuation date in the following year, the present value of the amortization payments due in the next six years would be added to the value of the plan's assets and that total would be compared to the plan's funding target. If a shortfall results, that would similarly be amortized in seven level payments. If there is no new shortfall, the plan would continue to pay the same amounts of remaining amortization payments as in the preceding year. This process would continue in each subsequent year.

For each year, a plan's sponsor would be required to contribute enough to cover that year's normal cost plus any amortization payments that are due to fund shortfalls. A plan sponsor could contribute more than the minimum required contribution, but merely that fact would not reduce the required payments for amortization of funding shortfalls. However, amortization payments would cease once the market value of plan assets exceeded the funding target. If the market value of plan assets exceeded the funding target by more than the normal cost, no plan contribution would be required for the year. The proposal would require a plan to make quarterly payments if its funding target was not fully covered by the value of its assets in the previous year. Fully funded plans would continue to have 8½ months after the end of the plan year to make their minimum required contributions.

Credit Balance

Under current law, a plan with a large credit balance may have no minimum required contribution even if the value of plan assets has dropped below the value of plan liabilities. A typical pension plan invested 60% in large cap common stocks and 40% in corporate bonds earned an investment return of -3.75% in 2001 and -9.16% in 2002.[19] This led to the market value of assets for many pension plans dropping below the value of plan liabilities. Nonetheless, if such a pension plan had a high enough credit balance in its Funding Standard Account at the beginning of the year, the plan sponsor was not required to make any pension contribution. The Administration's proposal would eliminate the credit balance so that it can no longer be used to offset the minimum required contribution.

Limiting Benefits and Distributions

In addition to keeping the present prohibition on a company in bankruptcy increasing its benefits, the proposal would freeze benefits and prevent additional accruals if the company's plan is not fully funded. The prohibition on benefit increases would also apply to any plan that was not funded at more than 80% of its target unless additional contributions were made to cover the cost of the amendment. In addition, continued accruals would be frozen for the plans of financially weak sponsors that were not funded at more than 60% of their target. These sponsors would also face restrictions against funding nonqualified deferred compensation arrangements for their top executives. These limits on benefit increases and accruals would not affect a plan in its first five years.

The prohibition on distributions in forms other than an annuity (e.g., lump sums) that applies to plans during a period of a liquidity shortfall would be extended under the proposal to all plans of companies in bankruptcy that are less than 100% funded, all plans that are funded at 60% or less, and to financially weak plans that are funded at 80% or less, based on the plan's funding target.

Increasing Deductible Contributions

The Administration's proposal allows companies to increase the amount of their deductible contributions by including two separate cushion amounts in their calculations. In addition to the amounts needed to raise the value of the plan assets to the sum of its funding target and that year's normal cost, plan sponsors could deduct contributions up to 30% of the plan's funding target and any increases that may be expected for future salary increases in a final salary plan or for benefit increases in a flat dollar plan. Finally, the deductible limit for the year would not be less than the sum of the plan's at-risk liability and its at-risk normal cost, regardless of whether the company is financially weak or not. The Full Funding Limitation would be eliminated.

Improving the Financial Position of the PBGC

The proposal would adjust the annual flat-rate premium for all plans from $19 to $30 per participant. This adjustment is based on the increase in the Social Security Administration's Average Wage Index since the $19 rate was set in 1991. This index is used to determine the annual increase in PBGC's maximum benefit guarantee and would be used to adjust the premium each year as well. The variable-rate premium of current law would be replaced by a risk-based premium that would be paid by any plan with assets less than its funding target. The same rate per dollar of underfunding would be paid by all plans. Plans with financially weak sponsors would be charged for each dollar of unfunded at-risk liability while plans with financially healthy sponsors would be charged for each dollar of unfunded ongoing liability. Note that the premium would be based on every dollar of unfunded liability (whether the benefits are vested or unvested) versus every dollar of unfunded vested benefits under current law. The rate for the risk-based premiums would be set periodically by the PBGC Board based on the goals of meeting expected future claims and eliminating the PBGC's current deficit over a reasonable period of time.

The proposal would also freeze the PBGC guarantee when a plan sponsor enters bankruptcy proceedings. If a plan terminates during these proceedings or within two years after the company emerges from bankruptcy, the PBGC guaranteed benefits would be based on plan provisions, salary and service records, and guarantee limits that were in effect on the date that the company entered bankruptcy. The plan administrator would be required to notify participants of these limitations put into effect by the bankruptcy. The proposal would amend federal bankruptcy laws to create an exemption that would allow the creation and perfection of a lien in favor of the PBGC against the plan sponsor for missed pension contributions, regardless of whether the lien is perfected before the company enters bankruptcy proceedings. The PBGC guarantee provisions would be amended to eliminate any coverage for unpredictable contingent event benefits, such as plant shutdown benefits.

Improving Disclosures

The proposal would require additional disclosures on a plan's Summary Annual Reports to participants (SAR) and to the government (Form 5500). On the Form 5500, plans would be required to disclose both ongoing and at-risk liability whether or not the sponsor was financially weak. The Schedule B actuarial statement would show the market value of the plan's assets in addition to the ongoing and at-risk liability. The SAR would show the funding status of the plan for each of the three last years as a percentage based on the ratio of the plan's assets to the appropriate funding target. The SAR would also include information on the financial health of the company and on the PBGC. The participant notice of underfunding required by §4011 of ERISA would be replaced by the SAR, which would now be due 15 days after the filing date for the Form 5500 and would be required to be sent to all participants regardless of the plan's funding status.

For plans that cover more than 100 participants and are required to make quarterly contributions because of their underfunding, the deadline for the Schedule B actuarial report would be moved up to the fifteenth day of the second month after the close of the plan year. Any additional contribution made for the plan year would be included on an amended Schedule B filed with the Form 5500.

Information filed with the PBGC pursuant to §4010 of ERISA would generally be available to the public. Confidential "trade secrets and commercial or financial information" would continue to fall under the Freedom of Information Act protections for corporate financial information.

YIELD CURVE PROPOSAL

Under current practice for the determination of present values, liabilities, and normal cost for a pension plan, a single interest rate is used to discount pension amounts payable at different points in the future. Under the Administration proposal, the ongoing liability, at-risk liability, and normal cost would be determined using a series of interest rates drawn from a yield curve for corporate bonds based on the timing of pension payments. This corporate bond yield curve would be issued monthly by the Secretary of the Treasury and would be based on the interest rates (averaged over 90 business days) for high quality corporate bonds (i.e., bonds rated AA) with varying maturities. **Figure 1** illustrates a yield curve.

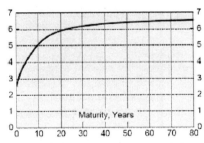

Source: Department of the Treasury, *Creating a Corporate Bond Spot Yield Curve for Pension Discounting,* from website [http://www.treas.gov/offices/economic-policy/reports/pension_yield curve_020705.pdf].

Figure 1. Spot Yield Curve — Corporate AA Bonds 12/30/04, Percent

We have provided below a simple example to illustrate the use of a yield curve for discounting. Consider a pension plan that covers four employees currently aged 25, 35, 45, and 55 which expects to make lump sum payments of $1,600,000, $800,000, $400,000, and $200,000 to these employees respectively when each reaches the retirement age of 65. **Table 1** shows the calculation of the present value of lump sum payments using spot rates from the yield curve in **Figure 1**. The total present value of lump sum payments using spot rates is $503,484.60.

Under prevalent actuarial practice, a single interest rate is used to discount future benefits. If a single rate of 6% was used to discount the same lump sum payments, the present value would be $531,244.50.[20]

**Table 1. Present Value Calculation Using
Spot Yield Curve, Corporate AA Bonds**

Employee current age	(a) Years to retirement	(b) Spot rate	(c) Lump sum payment at age 65	(d) = (c)*(1/(1+(b)^(a)) Present value of lump sum payment
55	10	5.02%	$200,000	$122,549.0
45	20	5.96%	$400,000	$125,666.9
35	30	6.33%	$800,000	$126,886.5
25	40	6.51%	$1,600,000	$128,382.1
			Total	$503,484.60

Source: Department of the Treasury, Spot rates from Appendix 2 of *Creating a Corporate Bond Spot Yield Curve for Pension Discounting*, [http://www.treas.gov/offices/economic-policy/reports/pension_ yieldcurve_020705.pdf]. Calculations by the Congressional Research Service (CRS).

Note: December 30, 2004 average of 90 business days.

The typical pension plan pays benefits as a stream of payments starting at retirement age, so that determining the present value of benefits using a yield curve is more complicated. However, large pension plans use sophisticated computer models to perform pension valuations and modification of these models to accommodate the yield curve should not be difficult.

Table 2 shows the values of life annuities payable at age 65 for different current ages using a single corporate bond rate versus a yield curve based on corporate bonds. The RP-2000 mortality table with 50% males and 50% females is used. In column (1) of **Table 2**, a single long-term corporate interest rate is used equal to the average yield on the Merrill Lynch U.S. Corporate Bond Index with AA ratings and time to maturity longer than 15 years. The average redemption yield on this index was 5.737% as of March 3, 2004, the date as of which the life annuity values in **Table 2** were determined. Column (2) uses a corporate bond yield curve computed using AA-rated financial bonds.

As **Table 2** illustrates, the present value of a life annuity starting at age 65 is higher for individuals aged 65 and 60 when a corporate bond yield curve is used instead of a single corporate bond rate. However, for individuals aged 50, 40, or 30, the use of a corporate bond yield curve for discounting instead of a single corporate bond rate reduces the value of the annuity.

The mechanism used to construct the corporate bond yield curve for the example in **Table 2** is somewhat different than the one proposed by Treasury. However, the message of **Table 2** applies just as much to the Treasury proposal. Use of a yield curve for discounting instead of a single interest rate, will generally increase the pension liabilities for older employees while it will reduce them for younger employees. The one exception is for situations when the yield curve is inverted, i.e., spot interest rates for longer durations are lower than spot interest rates for shorter durations. This has happened in the past but only on rare occasions.

Table 2. Life Annuity Values Starting at Age 65

Age	(1) Single corp. bond rate	(2) Corp. bond yield curve	Change (2)-(1)
65	11.22	11.73	4.55%
60	8.10	8.25	1.85%
50	4.42	3.89	-11.99%
40	2.46	1.94	-21.14%
30	1.38	1.01	-26.81%

Source: The Pension Forum, *Understanding the Corporate Bond Yield Curve*, by Höfling, Kiesel, and Löffler, Dec. 2004.

As a result, use of the yield curve will generally raise the contribution for a plan consisting of older participants as compared to an approach under which a single interest rate is used. Manufacturing companies such as the auto makers and auto suppliers tend to be comprised of older employees and will generally be required to make higher contributions under the yield curve proposal.

PROPOSED LEGISLATION

There are currently several comprehensive retirement security bills that include major provisions affecting defined benefit pension plans: S. 219, the

National Employee Savings and Trust Equity Guarantee Act of 2005 (NESTEG), introduced on January 31, 2005 by Senators Grassley and Baucus, H.R. 1960, and H.R. 1961, each titled the Pension Preservation and Savings Expansion Act of 2005 (PPSE), and each introduced on April 28, 2005 by Representatives Portman and Cardin respectively, and H.R. 2830, the Pension Protection Act of 2005, introduced on June 9, 2005 by Representative Boehner.[21] H.R. 2830 was ordered to be reported by the House Education and Workforce Committee on June 30. It is now under consideration by the House Ways and Means Committee where it may be folded into a larger retirement security bill. Other bills have also been introduced that would affect defined benefit plans and/or the PBGC. In April 2005, the House and Senate adopted a joint Budget Resolution that is likely to influence the direction of pension reform.

Replacement of Interest Rate on 30-Year Treasury Securities

Without legislative action, the interest rate used to value the current liability under current law would revert in 2006 to a rate based on yields of 30-year Treasury bonds.

S. 219

Under NESTEG, the 30-year Treasury rate would be replaced for 2006 by a permissible range that is not more than 10% below the weighted average of conservative long-term corporate bond rates during the four-year period ending on the last day before the beginning of the plan year. For the next five years, the yield curve method would be phased into the calculation at a rate of 20% per year until it is fully established in 2011. One or more simplified methods would be established by the Secretary of the Treasury for plans with no more than 100 participants. One of these simplified methods would also be permitted in calculating unfunded current liability for purposes of paying the variable rate premium to the PBGC in years after 2006. For plan years beginning in 2006, the interest rate would be the conservative long-term bond rate for the month before the plan year begins.

Under NESTEG, the yield curve method would also be phased in over five years to replace the 30-year Treasury rate in calculations to determine the present value of accrued benefits by those plans that offer the option of a lump-sum distribution. The interest rate used to determine maximum permissible benefits under a defined benefit plan would be the same 5.5% rate that was put in place for 2004 and 2005 by P.L. 108-218.

H.R. 2830

The Pension Protection Act includes a modified "yield curve" approach. The modified yield curve approach would incorporate the use of three separate interest rates based on the future date at which a pension plan's benefit obligations come due, as defined in three broad categories: liabilities due within five years, liabilities due in between five and 20 years, and liabilities due after 20 years and until the estimated end of the plan's obligations. The Pension Protection Act would require employers to use the three appropriate interest rates under the modified yield curve to also calculate lump sum distributions for participants. Under current law, interest rates used to calculate pension liabilities are "smoothed," or averaged, over four years. The Pension Protection Act would reduce the smoothing of interest rates for funding purposes to the maximum of the most recent three plan years using a weighted average (50% of the most recent plan year, 35% from the second year, and 15% in the third year). For determination of lump sums, the rates would be based on current bond yields rather than a three-year weighted average.

Other Funding Requirements

H.R. 2830

The Pension Protection Act would require employers to make sufficient and consistent contributions to ensure that a plan meets its funding target. For a plan above the 60% funded status, its funding target would be phased in from a 90% level at a rate of 2% per year to a 100% level after five years. If an employer's plan falls below a 60% funded status, its funding target would be based on the assumption that all participants would elect lump sums at the earliest opportunity and would include a loading factor. If a plan has a funding shortfall based on its funding target, the bill would require employers to make additional contributions to erase the shortfall over a seven-year period.

Under current law, a plan sponsor may "smooth" or average the appreciation or depreciation in plan assets over a period of up to five years. The Pension Protection Act would reduce the extent of allowed smoothing for assets to the maximum of the most recent three plan years using a weighted average (50% of the most recent plan year, 35% from the second year, and 15% in the third year). The smoothed value would be required to fall between 90% to 110% of the plan's fair market value.

The Pension Protection Act would prohibit employers from using credit balances to reduce plan contributions if their pension plans are funded at less than 80%.

Deduction Rules

S. 219

Under NESTEG, the maximum threshold for a deductible contribution to a plan would be raised to 130% of the plan's current liability. The overall limitation on deductions for contributions to a defined contribution plan by an employer who also sponsors a defined benefit plan would only apply in a case where such contributions exceed 6% of the amount otherwise paid to or accrued by the beneficiaries for that year. In determining the excise tax on nondeductible contributions, matching contributions would not be counted if they are nondeductible only because of the overall limitation.

H.R. 1960 and H.R. 1961

Under PPSE, the overall limitation on deductions for contributions to combined plans would be repealed. These bills would also deduct from the gross income of employees in the private sector any contributions they were required to make to a defined benefit plan. Most single-employer defined benefit pension plans do not require or permit contributions to the plan. Employee contributions for the few plans that allow such contributions are made on an after-tax basis under current law.

H.R. 2830

The Pension Protection Act would permit employers to make additional contributions up to a new higher maximum deductible of up to 150% of the plan's funding target (equivalent to the plan's current liability).

Limits on Benefits

S. 219

If a plan sponsor has debt rated below investment grade for two of the previous five years and if the plan assets have a fair market value that is less than 50% of current liability for vested benefits, then NESTEG would prohibit the plan from improving benefits or paying lump-sum distributions and no further benefits would accrue from additional service, age or salary growth. These prohibitions would be effective at the beginning of the next plan year (or of the next collective bargaining agreement). They would continue until the first day of the plan year in which the company's bond rating has been investment grade or the assets have exceeded 50% of the current liability for vested benefits for five years, as long as the assets will continue to exceed the 50% threshold after any increases are considered. Participants and beneficiaries, as well as the PBGC, would be notified at least 45 days before the start of the plan year that the plan is financially distressed, why it is so classified, and what restrictions would be in effect because of that.

H.R. 1960 and H.R. 1961

PPSE would apply a 50% golden parachute excise tax to any remuneration paid to an executive in excess of $1 million during a company's bankruptcy period defined as beginning on the date two years before the company declares bankruptcy and ending when it emerges from bankruptcy.

H.R. 2233 and S. 991

H.R. 2233 was introduced by Representative George Miller on May 10, 2005, while S. 991 was introduced by Senator Kennedy also on May 10, 2005. The Pension Fairness and Full Disclosure (PFFD) Act of 2005 would make a company's ability to provide nonqualified deferred compensation to its executives dependent on its providing adequate funding for its qualified plans for other workers.

H.R. 2830

The Pension Protection Act would prohibit employers and union leaders from increasing benefits or providing lump sum distributions if a pension plan is less than 80% funded unless the plan sponsor immediately makes the necessary contribution to fund the entire increase or payout. It would also prohibit further benefit accruals for plans with assets less than 60% funded status, which would effectively freeze the plan. The act would restrict the use of executive compensation arrangements if an employer has a severely underfunded plan. It would eliminate limitations on benefit increases to a pension plan if that plan meets the 100% funding threshold or more, including assets and existing credit balances.

The Pension Protection Act would require plans that become subject to these limitations to notify affected workers and retirees. In addition to letting workers know about the limits, this notice must alert workers when funding levels deteriorate and benefits already earned are in jeopardy.

PBGC Premiums

S. 219

With the goal of encouraging the establishment of defined benefit pension plans by small employers (100 or fewer participants), NESTEG would establish a lower PBGC premium structure for insuring new defined benefit plans of such employers. The annual PBGC flat-rate premium would be $5 per participant for the first five years of new plans sponsored by employers with no more than 100 employees on the first day of the plan year. A reduced variable-rate premium would be available for the first five years for all new plans. The percentage of the otherwise applicable rate to be paid by the new plan would be zero in the first year, 20% in the second year, 40% in the third year, 60% in the fourth year, and 80% in the fifth year. The variable-rate premium for plans sponsored by employers with no more than 25 employees on the first day of the plan year would be capped at $5 multiplied by the number of participants at the end of the preceding plan year.

H.R. 2830

The Pension Protection Act would raise flat-rate premiums employers pay to the PBGC but phase the increases in over time. For pension plans that are less than 80% funded, the bill would raise the flat per-participant rate premium from the current $19 to $30 over three years. For plans funded at more than 80%, the premium increase would be phased in over five years. The bill would index the flat-rate premium annually to worker wage growth thereafter. It would index the variable-rate premium, currently $9 per participant per $1,000 of underfunding, annually to worker wage growth.

Other Provisions Affecting the PBGC

S. 219

Under NESTEG, the 60-month phase-in of PBGC's guarantee of recent benefit increases in the case of a terminated plan would be extended to substantial owners (those who control more than 10% of the stock of a corporation) who are not majority owners (those who control 50% or more). The phase-in period for majority owners would be 10 years rather than the 30 years that it is for all substantial owners under current law. The rules regarding allocation of assets that apply to other participants would also be extended to substantial owners who are not majority owners.

Another provision of the NESTEG bill would accelerate the computation and payment of benefits attributable to recoveries the PBGC makes on its claims for unfunded benefit liabilities by moving back two years the five-year period it uses in determining its average recovery ratio. This ratio that in turn determines the portion of the recovered amounts to be allocated to participants would also be calculated for the amounts recovered from an employer for contributions owed to the plan. This provision would not take effect for large plans in which the loss of participants' benefits exceeds $20 million.

H.R. 2327 and S. 1158

H.R. 2327 was introduced by Representative George Miller on May 12, 2005 while S. 1158 was introduced by Senator Kennedy on May 26, 2005. These bills would impose a six-month moratorium beginning May 1, 2005 on terminations of plans in cases where the plan sponsor of a plan with unfunded termination liabilities of at least $1 billion is seeking reorganization in bankruptcy or insolvency proceedings. If enacted into law during this six-month period, they would also require the PBGC to cease any termination activities and restore the plan to its status prior to the proceedings. The Labor Appropriations bill H.R. 3010 was passed by the House on June 24, 2005. It would prohibit funds appropriated by the bill from being used by the PBGC to enforce or implement the settlement agreement dated April 22, 2005 between UAL Corporation and the PBGC related to the takeover by the PBGC of United's pension plans.

S. 685

S. 685 was introduced by Senator Akaka on March 17, 2005. It would require the PBGC to raise the amount of the guaranty for pilots required to retire at 60 by calculating the monthly benefit in the form of a life annuity beginning at that age instead of 65.

H.R. 2106 and S. 861

H.R. 2106 was introduced by Representative Tom Price on May 4, 2005 while S. 861 was introduced by Senator Isakson on April 20, 2005. The

Employee Pension Preservation Act of 2005 would allow airlines to spread their deficit reduction payments over 25 years while freezing benefits at the current levels with no additional accruals. If the plan is subsequently terminated, the PBGC's liability would be capped at the level it would have been on the first day of the plan year in which the special funding was put into effect.

Reporting and Disclosure

S. 219, H.R. 1960 and H.R. 1961

At least once every three years pension plan administrators would be required by both NESTEG and PPSE to furnish to each participant working for the plan sponsor a statement that is written in a manner that can be understood by the average plan participant. The statement shall include the total benefits accrued and any nonforfeitable benefits that have accrued, or the earliest date on which benefits will become nonforfeitable. Such a statement shall also be made available to participants once a year upon written request, and annual notice of this availability can serve as an alternative to the full report. The Secretary of Labor would be directed to provide one or more model benefit statements including the appropriate information in an understandable manner.

H.R. 2830

The Pension Protection Act would require plan sponsors to file Form 5500 within 275 days after the end of the plan year and would require plans to include more information on their Form 5500 filings. A plan's enrolled actuary must explain the basis for all plan retirement assumptions on the Schedule B of Form 5500. The Pension Protection Act would enhance Section 4010 disclosure requirements and make all Form 4010 information filed with the PBGC available to the public, except for sensitive corporate proprietary information. Specifically, the bill would require employers to provide certain additional information to workers and retirees within 90 days after Form 4010 is due, including notifying them (1) that a plan has made a Form 4010 filing for the year; (2) the aggregate amount of assets, liabilities, and funded ratio of the plan; (3) the number of plans maintained by the employer that are less than 75% funded; and (4) the assets, liabilities, and funded ratio for those plans that are 75% funded or less.

Within 90 days after the close of the plan year, the Pension Protection Act would require plans to notify workers and retirees of the actuarial value of assets and liabilities and the funded percentage of their plan. Such notice must also include the plan's funding policy and asset allocations based on percentage of overall plan assets. The bill would also require plans to provide the Summary Annual Report to workers and retirees within 15 days following the Form 5500 filing deadline.

H.R. 2233 and S. 991

PFFD would require a plan sponsor who eliminates or reduces future benefit accruals under a defined benefit plan or reduces future employer contributions under a defined contribution plan to fully disclose the details of the sponsor's executive compensation plans.

Studies

S. 219

S 219 calls for a study by the Secretary of the Treasury, the Secretary of Labor, and the Executive Director of the PBGC on ways to revitalize interest in defined benefit plans among employers with a report due in two years containing recommendations for legislative changes.

Age Discrimination and Cash-Balance Plan Provisions

H.R. 2830 would establish an age discrimination standard for all defined benefit plans that clarifies current law with respect to age discrimination requirements under ERISA on a prospective basis. It would prevent employers from reducing or eliminating vested benefits an employee has earned when converting to a cash-balance plan. It would eliminate age discrimination questions for plans where older workers' benefits are equal to or greater than those of similarly situated younger plan members.

Budget Reconciliation Process and Implications

At the end of April 2005, the House and the Senate adopted a joint Budget Resolution that assumed an increase in revenues from PBGC premiums of $6.6 billion over five years. This number is somewhat higher than the original Senate proposal of $5.3 billion, but considerably lower than the original House proposal of $18.1 billion.

Budget resolutions guide the budget reconciliation process by determining how much revenue congressional committees must raise from the federal programs they control, and how much lawmakers must reduce program spending. For the federal program budgets overseen by the House Education and the Workforce and the Senate HELP committees, the PBGC is a major source of revenue.

If the revenue required is not raised through higher PBGC premiums, the committees would be required to raise revenues or reduce outlays from other mandatory programs in their jurisdictions. Budget reconciliation bills are moved in a streamlined process.

ANALYSIS OF FORM 5500 DATA

An exhaustive analysis of the impact of reform proposals is beyond the scope of this report. However, in this section, we provide an assessment of the number of plans that might be affected by provisions of the Administration proposal related to the credit balance in the Funding Standard Account and the actuarial value of plan assets. We analyzed Form 5500 Schedule B filings for years 2001 and 2002 for plans covered by the PBGC in order to conduct our analysis. These are the latest years for which such data are available. We used data provided by the PBGC for our analysis. Our analysis indicated 29,315 plans for 2001 and 28,265 plans for 2002.[22] The PBGC as well as the Government Accountability Office (GAO) have conducted other analyses using large plans only.[23]

Credit Balance

Under the Administration proposal, use of the credit balance to reduce the minimum required contribution would be prohibited for all plans while under the Pension Protection Act, use of the credit balance would be banned for plans that are funded at less than 80%. We analyzed Form 5500 Schedule B data for years 2001 and 2002 to evaluate the prevalence of positive credit balances for pension plans and the extent to which positive credit balances contributed to the plan sponsor making no contributions to the plan. We did our analysis for all plans and also separately for underfunded plans.

Table 3. Prevalence of Positive
Credit Balance for Single-Employer Plans

Category of plans	Number of plans	
	2001	**2002**
All	29,315	28,265
Positive credit balance at beginning of year (BOY)	18,175 (62%)	17,455 (62%)
No employer contribution for year	8,988 (31%)	6,689 (24%)
No employer contribution for year and positive credit balance at BOY	5,998	4,274

Source: The Congressional Research Service (CRS) analysis of Form 5500 Schedule B data.
Note: Only plans covered by the PBGC and that had filed the Schedule B were considered.

As **Table 3** illustrates, for years 2001 as well as 2002, a substantial proportion (62%) of single-employer pension plans had a positive credit balance at the beginning of the plan year.[24] The proportion of plans with no employer contribution was 31% in 2001 and dropped somewhat to 24% in 2002. Of the plans with zero employer contribution, 67% had a positive credit balance at the beginning of 2001 while 64% had a positive credit balance at the beginning of 2002. The remaining plans would have been exempt from making a contribution on account of other reasons such as the application of the Full Funding Limit.

The rationale behind the proposal for the elimination of the credit balance is that a plan may be underfunded and yet not receive an employer contribution on account of application of a positive credit balance. **Table 4** examines the prevalence of underfunded pension plans with a positive credit balance. For purposes of **Table 4**, underfunded pension plans were defined as those plans for which the fair market value of plan assets was lower than the Current Liability as of the beginning of the plan year.

As **Table 4** illustrates, the proportion of underfunded pension plans was 52% at the beginning of the 2001 plan year, and increased to 58% at the beginning of the 2002 plan year. The proportion of underfunded plans that received no employer contributions for the year was 17% for 2001 and a somewhat lower 13% for 2002. Of the underfunded plans with no employer contribution, 71% had a positive credit balance at the beginning of 2001 while 68% had a positive credit balance at the beginning of 2002, which presumably was the major reason for the plan not receiving an employer contribution for the year.[25]

Table 4. Prevalence of Positive Credit Balance
for Underfunded Single-Employer Plans

Category of plans	Number of plans	
	2001	2002
All	29,315	28,265
Current liability > Market value of assets	15,299 (52%)	16,253 (58%)
Current liability > Market value of assets but no employer contribution for year	2,579	2,074
Current liability > Market value of assets, no employer contribution for year and positive credit balance at BOY	1,829	1,417

Source: The Congressional Research Service (CRS) analysis of Form 5500 Schedule B data.
Note: Only plans covered by the PBGC and that had filed the Schedule B were considered.

Interest on the credit balance is credited at the rate assumed by the plan actuary for funding purposes. **Table 5** shows the variation in the assumed interest rate for the plan year 2001.

The average interest rate assumed was 7.1% for plan year 2001 and 7.0% for plan year 2002. According to the PBGC, the average assumed interest rate tends to be higher for larger plans. For the 2001 and 2002 plan years, for example, PBGC analysis indicates that the average assumed interest rate for plans with 100 or more participants was 8.0%. A typical pension plan invested 60% in large-cap stocks and 40% in long-term corporate bonds would have earned -3.75 % in 2001 and -9.16% in 2002.[26]

Table 5. Funding Interest Assumption for Single-Employer Pension
Plans

Interest rate	Percent of plans	
	2001	2002
<6%	13%	17%
> or = 6%, < 7%	26%	24%
> or = 7%, < 8%	26%	25%
> or = 8%, < 9%	30%	30%
> or = 9%	5%	4%

Source: The Congressional Research Service (CRS) analysis of Form 5500 Schedule B data.
Note: Only plans covered by the PBGC and that had filed the Schedule B were considered.

Some have suggested the following alternatives to the elimination of the credit balance:

(1) Allow use of the credit balance in the FSA but accrue interest on it at the actual rate earned by the pension trust for the year rather than the long-term interest rate assumed by the plan's actuary.

(2) Allow use of the credit balance in the FSA but do not accrue interest on it.

Appendix 2 illustrates the effect of these alternate approaches on a hypothetical plan's minimum required contribution and funded status. The illustration in the Appendix shows that the change in the minimum required contribution on account of the above two approaches is small compared to the impact of disallowing use of the credit balance.

Use of Fair Market Value instead of Actuarial Value

Under current law, the minimum required and maximum deductible contribution rules allow use of the actuarial value of assets rather than the fair market value of assets. In years in which the investment return on plan assets is negative, the actuarial value for a plan may be higher than the market value of assets since it may defer the recognition of capital losses. This was the case for many plans in years 2000, 2001, and 2002, when the S&P 500 returns were -9.19%, -11.87%, and -22.10% respectively. The result for such plans was that the funding requirements were lower than would have resulted from use of the fair market value of plan assets.

Under the Administration proposal, the fair market value of assets would be used to determine the funding requirements as well as the unfunded liability for calculation of the variable rate PBGC premiums. Under the Pension Protection Act, an actuarial value of assets based on less smoothing than under current law would be employed. **Table 6** below shows the relationship between actuarial value and fair market value based on data obtained from Form 5500 filings.

In 2001, there were more plans with an actuarial value greater than the market value (17%) than plans with an actuarial value lower than the market value (11%). This pattern was even more pronounced in 2002. Twenty-seven percent of plans had an actuarial value greater than the market value while 6% of plans had an actuarial value lower than the market value.

**Table 6. Ratio of Actuarial Value to Market
Value for Single-Employer Pension Plans**

AV/MV as of valuation date	Percent of plans	
	2001	2002
< 0.9	2%	1%
> or = 0.9, < 1	9%	5%
1	66%	63%
> 1, < or = 1.1	12%	10%
> 1.1, < or = 1.2	5%	17%
MV = 0	5%	5%

Source: The Congressional Research Service (CRS) analysis of Form 5500 Schedule B data.
Note: Only plans covered by the PBGC and that had filed the Schedule B were considered.

REACTIONS TO ADMINISTRATION PROPOSAL

While some have applauded the Administration proposal for taking a broad, comprehensive approach to pension reform rather than providing temporary solutions, business as well as labor have raised several objections.[27] These include:

- *Volatility* — Elimination of smoothing in the determination of the interest rate and asset value and the ban on use of the credit balance will result in far greater volatility in the minimum required pension contribution.
- *Credit Balance* — Elimination of the credit balance is not fair to employers that have made plan contributions in excess of the minimum required amounts in the past with the expectation that these could be used to reduce future contributions. Also, elimination of the credit balance will create a disincentive for making plan contributions in excess of the minimum required amount.
- *Counter-Cyclical* — Required contributions and PBGC premium increases would be highest for companies experiencing financial difficulty who can least afford them. This could lead to more bankruptcies, plant closings, and layoffs.
- *Access to Surplus Assets* — Although the Administration proposal will raise the maximum deductible contribution ceiling, companies will be reluctant to make higher contributions unless they are

allowed to access "super-surpluses" for legitimate purposes such as payment of other employee benefits.

- *Disruption of Capital Markets* — The lack of asset and liability smoothing in the new funding rules may drive employers to move pension investments from stocks to bonds in order to reduce volatility. This is likely to result in a decline in stock prices as well as in interest rates offered on bonds.

- *PBGC Premiums Too High* — Proposed premiums will be too high, especially for a company experiencing financial difficulty. This, combined with higher funding requirements for such companies, could lead to many employers freezing or terminating their defined benefit pension plans.

- *PBGC Powers to Set Premiums* — At a minimum, Congress should set limits on how large the PBGC premium increases can be and how well PBGC should be funded.

- *Transition* — A transition period of three years or more is needed to allow financial markets to accommodate pension funds' shift from stocks to bonds.

- *Public Policy Does Not Favor Defined Benefit Plans* — With lower tax rates for capital gains and stock dividends, employers have little incentive to provide pension benefits as compared to cash compensation. One suggestion is that the Congress tax pension distributions at the same rates as capital gains and stock dividends in order to provide a level playing field.

The Administration's response to business and labor objections was included in several testimonies offered on the Hill.[28] The Pension Protection Act (H.R. 2830) incorporates several elements of the Administration proposal but in a modified form so that the impact on plan sponsors will generally be lower.

APPENDIX 1. MEASURES OF PENSION LIABILITY

Current pension law requires calculation of at least four separate measures of pension liability that are used for different purposes. Not only are these defined differently, but a different interest rate is used for valuing each liability. **Table 7** highlights the differences between these measures of liability.

Table 7. Measures of Liability Under Pension Law

Liability	Definition	Uses	Interest rate	Authorization and rationale
Accrued Liability (AL)	Portion of Present Value (PV) of total benefits associated with the past under the actuarial cost method chosen for funding.	AL less Actuarial Value of assets is spread over a number of years specified by law in calculating the minimum required and maximum deductible pension contribution.	Rate chosen by plan's actuary such that along with other assumptions it represents his best estimate of anticipated plan experience.	ERISA (1974) required systematic funding of the unfunded AL. It provided flexibility in the choice of actuarial cost method and interest rate.
Current Liability (CL)	PV of benefits earned to date by employees based on service and compensation to date. Includes liability for non vested benefits.	Used to determine overrides to minimum required and maximum deductible contributions determined under the plan's funding method.	Interest rate must fall between 90%-100% of four year weighted average of interest rates on long- term corporate bonds (for 2004 and 2005).	Instituted by OBRA 87 to bring more uniformity to determination of minimum required and maximum deductible contributions.
Present Value (PV) of vested benefits	Liability for retiree pension benefits and benefits earned to date by vested active participants based on service and compensation to date.	PV of vested benefits less actuarial value of plan assets used to determine the variable rate PBGC premiums payable by the plan.	85% of interest rate on long- term corporate bonds (for 2004 and 2005).	Variable rate premiums instituted in 1987 in order to charge higher premiums to higher risk plans.
Termination Liability	PV of benefits payable to plan participants if plan were to be terminated. Includes vested as well as unvested benefits.	Must be disclosed to the P B G C b y employers with plans that have aggregate unfunded present value of vested benefits greater than $50 million.	Rate used by private insurers to price immediate annuities for retirees and deferred annuities for active employees. This is usually considerably lower than rates used to determine other types of liabilities.	Authorized by Section 4010 of ERISA. Provides PBGC information for determining its exposure for reasonably possible and probable terminations.

Source: The Congressional Research Service (CRS).

Two other measures of pension liability are used in accounting disclosure. Publicly traded companies must file annual reports under Securities and Exchange Commission requirements that include disclosure of the funded status of pension plans. The funded status is based on a measure of pension liability called the *Projected Benefit Obligation (PBO)*. The PBO as of a certain date is the actuarial present value of all benefits attributed by the pension benefit formula to employee service rendered prior to that date. The PBO is measured using assumptions as to future compensation levels if the pension benefit formula is based on those future compensation levels. In addition, underfunded pension plans must disclose the *Accumulated Benefit Obligation (ABO)*.[29] The ABO as of a certain date is the actuarial present value of all benefits attributed by the pension benefit formula to employee service rendered prior to that date and based on employee service and compensation prior to that date. The ABO differs from the PBO in that it includes no assumption about future compensation levels. The interest rate used to determine the PBO and ABO is typically the rate on high quality long-term bonds during the period to maturity of pension benefits.

APPENDIX 2. ILLUSTRATIVE IMPACT OF ALTERNATE CREDIT BALANCE PROPOSALS ON MINIMUM REQUIRED CONTRIBUTION AND FUNDED RATIO

We have determined in the example below a hypothetical plan's minimum required contribution under the following alternatives:

(a) Current law.
(b) Administration proposal — No credit balance carryover in the Funding Standard Account.
(c) Allow use of the credit balance in the FSA but accrue interest on it at the actual rate earned by the pension trust for the year rather than the interest rate assumed by the plan's actuary. This approach is used under H.R. 2830 but only for plans that are not underfunded.
(d) Allow use of the credit balance in the FSA but do not accrue interest on it. This approach would be a possible compromise between current law and the Administration proposal.

In addition, we have illustrated for the four alternatives the effect on the plan assets and the funded ratio, assuming that the employer makes a contribution to the plan equal to the minimum required contribution. For purposes of this Appendix, we have defined the funded ratio as the ratio of the plan's current liability to the market value of plan assets.

The example chosen for this illustration was modeled after airline pension plans that were underfunded in recent years, yet made no pension contribution on account of a high credit balance. We used available information from the 2002 Schedule B of the Form 5500 for certain airline pension plans to guide the use of plan characteristics chosen for the illustration. However we did not exactly match entries from any one airline pension plan's Schedule B in order to keep the illustration simple and protect confidentiality. Consider a plan with the characteristics shown in **Table 8**.

Table 8. Plan Characteristics for Illustration

Market value of assets — beginning of year (BOY)	$20,000,000
Current liability	$22,000,000
Benefit payout for year	$2,000,000
Current liability — end of year	$22,000,000
Credit balance at BOY	$700,000
Interest earned for year	-9.16%
Interest assumed for year	9.0%

Source: Congressional Research Service (CRS) assumptions.

Table 9 shows the development of the Funding Standard Account and the minimum required contribution under alternatives (a), (b), (c), and (d). Under all four alternatives, lines (1), (2), (3), and (4), which represent charges to the FSA, are identical. However, the values in line (5) are different depending on whether the alternative allows the credit balance to be used as an offset. Also, the values in line (6) are different depending on the rate used to credit interest on the credit balance.

As **Table 9**, Alternative (a) illustrates, under current law, the large credit balance of $700,000 at the beginning of the plan year leads to no pension contribution being required for the year. Under the Administration proposal —Alternative (b), the credit balance would not be recognized in developing the minimum required contribution. This results in the minimum required contribution increasing from $0 to $719,400. If the credit balance is taken into account in the calculations, but interest is accrued on it at the earned rate of -9.16% rather than the assumed rate of 9% — Alternative (c), the minimum required contribution would be a relatively low $83,520. Finally, if the credit balance is taken into account in the calculations, but no interest is accrued on it — Alternative (d), the minimum required contribution would be an even lower amount of $19,400.

Table 9. Minimum Required Contributions
under Alternate Credit Balance Proposals

	Current law (a)	Administration proposal - No credit balance (b)	Interest on credit balance at earned rate (c)	No interest on credit balance (d)
Charges to funding standard account				
(1) Normal cost as of Jan. 1	$360,000	$360,000	$360,000	$360,000
(2) Amortization charges as of Jan 1.	$300,000	$300,000	$300,000	$300,000
(3) Interest = .09 ((1)+(2))	$59,400	$59,400	$59,400	$59,400
(4) Total charges = (1)+(2)+(3)	$719,400	$719,400	$719,400	$719,400
Credits to funding standard account				
(5) Prior year credit balance	$700,000	$0	$700,000	$700,000
(6) Interest	$63,000	$0	($64,120)	$0
(7) Total credits = (5)+(6)	$763,000	$0	$635,880	$700,000
Minimum required contribution = (4)-(7)	$0	$719,400	$83,520	$19,400

Source: Congressional Research Service (CRS) calculations.

Note: Interest on Normal Cost and Amortization charges under all four alternatives is calculated at the assumed rate of 9%.

Table 10 develops the plan assets at the end of the plan year if the employer makes plan contributions equal to the minimum required contributions under alternatives (a), (b), (c), and (d) respectively as developed in **Table 9**. **Table 10** also shows the effect on the funded ratio under the different alternatives. If no contribution is made as permitted under current law — Alternative (a), the market value of assets would drop from $20 million at the beginning of the year to $16.17 million at the end of the year, thereby reducing the funded ratio from 0.91 at the beginning of the year to 0.73 at the end of the year. Under the Administration proposal — Alternative (b), the contribution would be $719, 400. This helps offset some of the asset loss and results in a funded ratio of 0.77 at the end of the year. If the employer makes plan contributions as required under Alternative (c) or Alternative (d), plan assets at the end of the year would be higher than under current law, but lower than under the Administration proposal. As a result, the funded ratio at the end of the year under either Alternative (c) or Alternative (d) is 0.74, somewhat better than under current law and considerably lower than the one produced under the Administration proposal.

Table 10. Plan Assets and Funded Ratios
under Alternate Credit Balance Proposals

	Current law (a)	Administration proposal No credit balance (b)	Interest on credit balance at earned rate (c)	No interest on credit balance (d)
(1) Market value of assets — BOY	$20,000,000	$20,000,000	$20,000,000	$20,000,000
(2) Current liability BOY	$22,000,000	$22,000,000	$22,000,000	$22,000,000
Funded ratio — BOY = (1)/(2)	0.91	0.91	0.91	0.91
(3) Contribution	$0	$719,400	$83,520	$19,400
(4) Benefit payout	$2,000,000	$2,000,000	$2,000,000	$2,000,000
(5) Market value of assets — end of year = (1)*(1-.0916)+(3)-(4)	$16,168,000	$16,887,400	$16,251,520	$16,187,400
(6) Current liability — end of year	$22,000,000	$22,000,000	$22,000,000	$22,000,000
Funded ratio — end of year = (5)/(6)	0.73	0.77	0.74	0.74

Source: Congressional Research Service (CRS) calculations.

The impact of the alternate credit balance proposals on the minimum required contribution and funded ratio will depend on values of specific variables including the interest rate earned by plan assets, actuarial interest assumption, the credit balance at the beginning of the year, market value of plan assets at the beginning of the year, and current liability at the beginning and end of the year. This Appendix is intended to illustrate the impact of alternate proposals on a hypothetical plan rather than provide an exhaustive analysis of the impact of alternate proposals on the universe of plans with a wide range of varying characteristics. However, we would expect that the impact on the minimum required contribution of recognizing the credit balance with zero interest or market rate of interest would generally be small relative to disallowing use of the credit balance.

REFERENCES

[1]   The PBGC's assets consist of revenues from premiums charged on pension plans that it insures, assets of terminated pension plans, and any asset recoveries from plan sponsors of terminated pension plans.

The PBGC assets also include investment income on PBGC revenues. The PBGC's liabilities consist of the present value of the benefits payable by the PBGC for participants in terminated pension plans, plans whose termination is pending, and probable terminations. The PBGC receives no appropriations from Congress. For additional information on the PBGC's financial status, see CRS Report RL32702, *Can the Pension Benefit Guaranty Corporation be Restored to Financial Health?*, by Neela K Ranade.

[2] See page 5 of CBO testimony *Defined-Benefit Pension Plans: Current Problems and Future Challenges,* before the Senate Finance Committee, June 7, 2005, at [http://www.cbo.gov/ftpdocs/64xx/doc6 414/06-07-PBGC.pdf].

[3] For more details see Joint Committee on Taxation, *Present Law and Background Relating to Employer-Sponsored Defined Benefit Pension Plans and the Pension Benefit Guaranty Corporation ("PBGC")*, JCX-03-05, Feb. 28, 2005; and Department of Labor, *Strengthen Funding for Single-Employer Pension Plans*, Feb. 7, 2005.

[4] *PBGC Performance and Accountability Report-Fiscal Year 2004*, p. 8.

[5] United Airlines and US Airways, for example, made no contributions for several years preceding termination of their pilots' pension plans, even though the plans were severely underfunded. See PBGC testimony before the House Subcommittee on Transportation and Infrastructure, June 22, 2005 at [http://www.pbgc.gov/news/speeches/ testimony_062205.htm].

[6] A plan sponsor may make a contribution in excess of the maximum deductible limit. However, this would be subject to an excise tax.

[7] The actuarial funding methods listed on the 2004 Schedule B of the Form 5500 are attained age normal, entry age normal, accrued benefit, aggregate, frozen initial liability, individual level premium, and the individual aggregate method.

[8] For the 2001 and prior plan years, the interest rate used to determine the current liability was required to fall between 90%-105% of the four-year weighted average of rates on long-term Treasury bonds. Under the terms of the Job Creation and Worker Assistance Act of 2002 (P.L. 107-147), the permissible range was changed to 90%-120% of such weighted average for plan years 2002 and 2003.

[9] For plan years 2002 and 2003,the FFL was the excess if any of the lesser of (1)(a) accrued liability under the plan including normal cost or (b) the applicable percentage of the current liability (including current liability normal cost), over the lesser of (2)(c) market value of plan

assets or (d) actuarial value of plan assets. The applicable percentage was defined as 165% for 2002 and 170% for 2003. However, the FFL could not be lower than the excess if any of 90% of the current liability (including current liability normal cost) over the actuarial value of plan assets.

[10] The additional funding requirements were enacted by OBRA-87 and amended by the Retirement Protection Act of 1994 to address demands on the PBGC insurance system as a result of terminations of underfunded pension plans.

[11] However, the requirement does not apply if the actuarial value of the plan's assets is between 80% and 90% of current liability, provided that the plan's assets were at least 90% of current liability in two consecutive years out of the last three years.

[12] For a more complete description of additional funding requirements, see *Present Law and Background Relating to Employer-Sponsored Defined Benefit Pension Plans and the Pension Benefit Guaranty Corporation ("PBGC")*, JCX-03-05, Feb. 28, 2005.

[13] For more information, see CRS Report RS21717, *H.R. 3108: The Pension Funding Equity Act*, by Patrick Purcell and Paul Graney.

[14] IRC Section 412(l)(7)(C)(ii)(II) allows the Secretary of the Treasury to specify an updated mortality table to be used by pension plans for the determination of the current liability and the vested benefits. 29 CFR§4006.4 states that when the mortality table is updated, the fair market value of assets rather than the actuarial value of assets must be used to determine the unfunded vested benefits.

[15] This phase-in period is 30 years beginning with participation in the plan for a substantial owner, i.e., one who owns more than 10% of the company.

[16] See CRS Report RL32960 *Age Restrictions for Airline Pilots: Revisiting the FAA's 'Age 60 Rule'* by Bart Elias.

[17] Two or more companies are said to form a controlled group if the parent corporation owns at least 80% of the stock in each company.

[18] For more details see Joint Committee on Taxation, *Present Law and Background Relating to Employer-Sponsored Defined Benefit Pension Plans and the Pension Benefit Guaranty Corporation ("PBGC")*, JCX-03-05, Feb. 28, 2005; Department of Labor, *Strengthen Funding for Single-Employer Pension Plans*, Feb. 7, 2005; Department of Labor, *Fact Sheet: The Bush Administration's Plan for Strengthening Retirement Security;* and Assistant Secretary of Treasury Mark J.

Warshawsky's testimony before the Senate Special Committee on Aging, Apr. 12, 2005.

[19] Common stocks assumed to track the S&P 500 stock index and corporate bonds assumed to track the Lehman Brothers Aggregate Bond Index.

[20] $0 \quad 1,600,000*(1/1.06)^{\wedge}40+800,000*(1/1.06)^{\wedge}30+400,000*(1/1.06)^{\wedge}20+ 200,000*(1/1.06)^{\wedge}10$.

[21] For more on H.R. 2830 see CRS Report RS22179, *H.R. 2830: The Pension Protection Act of 2005*, by Patrick Purcell.

[22] Table S-31 of PBGC's *Pension Insurance Data Book 2004* shows the number of single-employer plans covered by the PBGC to be 32,954 for 2001 and 31,229 for 2002. However, not all of these are required to file Schedule B forms.

[23] Analysis of the 100 largest single-employer defined benefit pension plans is available in the transcript of GAO's testimony before the Committee on the Budget, House of Representatives, *Private Pensions: The Pension Benefit Guaranty Corporation and Long-Term Budgetary Challenges,* GAO-05-772T.

[24] If only large plans are considered the proportion of plans with a positive credit balance at the beginning of the 2002 plan year would be even larger. According to the PBGC, of all plans considered for their PIMS Model, 86% had a positive credit balance at the beginning of the 2002 plan year. The 1998 Pension Insurance Data Book states that the PIMS data base has approximately 400 pension plans, sponsored by about 250 firms, which represent about 50% of liabilities and underfunding in the defined benefit plan system. These are among the largest plans in the defined benefit system.

[25] Some of the plans may not have received an employer contribution for other reasons such as the application of the Full Funding Limitation.

[26] Common stocks assumed to track the S&P 500 stock index and bonds assumed to track the Lehman Brothers Aggregate Bond Index.

[27] See for example, *Funding Our Future: A Safe and Sound Approach to Defined Benefit Pension Plan Funding Reform* by the American Benefits Council, at [http://www.americanbenefitscouncil.org/documents/fundingpaper021604.pdf] and testimony by United Auto Workers before the Senate Committee on Health, Education, Labor and Pensions on April 26, 2005, at [http://help.senate.gov/ testimony /t269_tes.html].

[28] See for example GAO testimony before the House Committee on the Budget, *Private Pensions: The Pension Benefit Guaranty Corporation*

and Long-Term Budgetary Challenges, June 9, 2005, at [http://www.gao.gov/new.items/d05772t.pdf]; PBGC testimony before the House Subcommittee on Transportation and Infrastructure, June 22, 2005, at [http://www.pbgc.gov/news/speeches/testimony_062205.htm]; CBO testimony before the Senate Committee on the Budget, *The Pension Benefit Guaranty Corporation: Financial Condition, Potential Risks, and Policy Options*, June 15, 2005, at [http://www.cbo.gov/ftpdocs/64xx/doc6426/06-15-PBGC.pdf].

[29] For more information on the PBO and ABO, see *Statement of Financial Accounting Standards No. 87: Employers' Accounting for Pensions* by the Financial Accounting Standards Board.

In: Pensions: Reform, Protection and Health Insurance ISBN: 1-59454-704-1
Editor: Leo A. Felton, pp. 43-52   © 2006 Nova Science Publishers, Inc.

Chapter 2

H.R. 2830: THE PENSION PROTECTION ACT OF 2005[*]

Patrick Purcell

SUMMARY

On June 30, 2005, the House Committee on Education and the Workforce favorably reported H.R. 2830 (Boehner), *The Pension Protection Act of 2005.* As amended by the Committee, the bill would:

- Reform the funding rules for both single-employer and multiemployer defined benefit pensions,
- Require sponsors to disclose more information about pension finances,
- Restrict benefit payments and benefit accruals in underfunded plans,
- Increase the premiums that plan sponsors pay to the Pension Benefit Guaranty Corporation (PBGC), which insures defined benefit plans, and
- Clarify, prospectively, that cash balance pension plans do not ordinarily violate the legal prohibition on age discrimination in employee benefits.

---

[*] Excerpted from CRS Report RS22179 Updated July 18, 2005.

FUNDING REQUIREMENTS FOR
SINGLE-EMPLOYER PENSION PLANS

The *Pension Protection Act* would increase funding requirements for defined benefit pension plans and shorten the period over which funding shortfalls must be eliminated.[1] In general, plans would be required to fund 100% of their "funding target" which under current law is referred to as the plan's "current liability." The funding target would be the present value of all benefits — including early retirement benefits — that plan participants have earned as of the beginning of the plan year. The plan would have to amortize (pay off with interest) any funding shortfalls over seven years. Under current law, a plan's unfunded liability can be amortized over periods of up to 30 years in some circumstances. Under the bill, a plan's funding requirement in any year would be the present value of the benefits expected to be earned during the year by all active participants (called the "normal cost" of the plan) plus payments to amortize over seven years any pre-existing unfunded liability, less any permissible credit balance for prior contributions. The 100% percent funding target would be phased in over five years, as follows:

Year	Funding target (Percent of liabilities)
2006	92%
2007	94%
2008	96%
2009	98%
2010	100%

Plans with assets equal to less than 60% of the plan's liabilities (less than "60% funded") would be considered "at-risk" of default, and would be required to use more conservative actuarial assumptions in determining plan liability. Under the required actuarial assumptions, the plan sponsor would have to calculate the plan's current liability as if all participants would choose the retirement date and form of distribution that would be most costly to the plan. In addition, a "loading factor" of 4% of the plan's liabilities plus $700 per participant would be added to their required contribution. A plan's "at-risk" status would be based on the plan's ratio of assets to liabilities. In determining the ratio of assets to liabilities and calculating the loading factor, plans would use "regular" liabilities (calculated without assuming that everyone would take the most expensive benefit and without the load charges). The additional funding requirements for at-risk plans would be phased in at 20% per year after a plan enters at-risk status.

VALUATION OF ASSETS AND LIABILITIES

Under current law, a plan sponsor can determine the value of a plan's assets using "actuarial valuations." Actuarial valuations of plan assets can differ from the current market value of those assets. For example, in an actuarial valuation, the plan's investment returns may be averaged — or "smoothed" — over a five-year period, and the average asset value may range from 80% to 120% of the assets' fair market value. This "smoothing" is permitted because pension plans are considered long-term commitments, and smoothing reduces volatility in the measurement of plan liabilities and assets that can be caused by year-to-year fluctuations in interest rates and the rate of return on investments. Smoothing of interest rates and asset values therefore reduces the year-to-year volatility in the plan sponsor's required minimum contributions to a defined benefit pension plan. H.R. 2830 would narrow the range for actuarial valuations to 90% to 110% of the fair market value of assets and reduce the maximum smoothing period from five years to three years.

Pension plan liabilities — the pensions owed to participants and survivors — extend many years into the future. Determining whether the plan is adequately funded requires converting this long-term stream of pension payments into an equivalent lump sum, which is essentially the amount that would be needed today to pay off those liabilities all at once. This lump sum — representing the "present value" of the plan's liabilities — is then compared to the value of the plan's assets. An underfunded plan is one in which the value of the plan's assets falls short of the present value of its liabilities by more than the percentage allowed under law. Converting a future stream of payments (or income) into a present value requires the future payments (or income) to be "discounted" using an appropriate interest rate. Other things being equal, the *higher* the interest rate, the *smaller* the present value of the future payments (or income), and vice versa.

Under the bill, plan sponsors would determine the funding target (the present value of the plan's liabilities) using three interest rates, which would be based on when the benefits are projected to be paid: in less than five years, in 5 to 20 years, or in more than 20 years. The Secretary of the Treasury would determine the three rates, which would be derived from a "yield curve" of investment-grade corporate bonds.[2] Interest rates would be averaged over a three-year period under a weighting formula using 50% of the rate from the most recent plan year, 35% of the rate from the previous plan year and 15% from the plan year before that. The yield curve would be phased in during the 2006 and 2007 plan years, and become fully effective for the 2008 plan year. This methodology would permanently replace the four-year average of corporate bond rates established under P.L. 108-218, which expires with plan years ending after 2005.

CONTRIBUTION LIMITS AND CREDIT BALANCES

H.R. 2830 would allow plan sponsors to contribute more to their pension plans than they can under current law. It would set the maximum tax-deductible contribution at 150% of the plan's funding target (150% of the plan's current liability).[3] Within certain limits, sponsors would be able to offset required current contributions with previous contributions. However, using these so-called "credit balances" to offset required contributions would be permitted only in plans that are at least 80% funded and only after subtracting pre-enactment credit balances from plan assets. Credit balances also would have to be adjusted for investment gains and losses since the date of the original contribution that created the credit balance.

LUMP-SUM DISTRIBUTIONS

By law, defined benefit pensions must offer participants the option to receive their accrued benefits in the form of an annuity — a series of monthly payments guaranteed for life. Increasingly, however, defined benefit plans also have offered participants the option to take their accrued benefits as a single lump sum at the time they separate from the employer. The amount of a lump-sum distribution from a defined benefit pension is inversely related to the interest used to calculate the present value of the benefit that has been accrued under the plan: the higher the interest rate, the smaller the lump-sum and vice versa. Under current law, lump-sum distributions are calculated using the average interest rate on 30-year Treasury bonds. The interest rate on long-term Treasury securities has historically been lower than the average interest rate on long-term investment-grade corporate bonds because bond markets generally consider U.S. Treasury securities to be free of the risk of default. The Treasury

Department stopped issuing the 30-year bond in 2001, and the interest rate on bonds that have not yet been redeemed has fallen as the supply of bonds has shrunk. (Bond prices and interest rates are inversely related. As bond prices rise, their yields fall.)

H.R. 2830 would require plan sponsors to calculate lump-sum distributions using three interest rates based on investment-grade corporate bonds. As a result, participants of different ages would have their lump sum distributions calculated using different interest rates. Other things being equal, lump-sum distributions paid to workers nearer to retirement would be calculated using a lower interest rate than would be used for younger workers. As a result, all else being equal, an older worker would receive a larger lump-sum than a similarly situated younger worker. The interest rates used to calculate lump sums would be based on *current* bond rates rather than the three-year *weighted average* rate used to calculate the plan's funding target (current liability). The new rules for calculating lump sums would be phased-in over five years.

PBGC PREMIUMS FOR SINGLE-EMPLOYER PLANS

The Pension Benefit Guaranty Corporation (PBGC) was established by the Employee Retirement Income Security Act of 1974 (ERISA) to insure pension benefits under defined benefit pension plans. The PBGC is funded by premiums paid by plan sponsors and investment returns on the assets held in its trust fund. It receives no appropriations from Congress. The PBGC does not have the legal authority to set its own premiums, which are set in law by Congress. The PBGC has had to take over a number of large underfunded plans in recent years, and it reported a deficit of $23.3 billion at the end of 2004, raising concerns that the agency may require a taxpayer-financed "bailout" at some point in the future. The PBGC receives two types of premiums from plans sponsored by individual employers: a per-capita premium of $19 per year that is charged to all single-employer defined benefit plans, and a variable premium equal to $9 per $1,000 of underfunding (0.9%) charged to underfunded plans.

H.R. 2830 would raise the base annual PBGC premium from $19 to $30 per participant. The $30 premium would be phased in beginning in 2007, on a schedule based on the plan's funded status. For plans that are at least 80% funded, the higher premium would be phased in over five years. In plans that are less than 80% funded, the higher premium would be phased in over three years. The premium then would be indexed to average national wage growth.

The act would also increase the variable-rate premium (to be renamed the "risk-based premium") of $9 per $1,000 of underfunding by indexing it to the rate of growth of average wages beginning in 2008. Unlike current law, a plan would not be exempted from the risk-based premium if it was not underfunded in any two consecutive years out of the previous three years. The risk-based premium would be assessed on all underfunded plans, regardless of the plan's funding status in earlier years.

LIMITS ON BENEFITS IN UNDERFUNDED PLANS

H.R. 2830 would limit certain forms of benefit payments and the accrual of new benefits in underfunded plans. Plans funded at less than 80% could not pay lump-sum distributions and could not increase benefits without first fully funding the new benefits. In plans less than 60% funded, benefits would be "frozen" and no new benefits could be earned under the plan. Participants would have to be notified of these restrictions on benefits. An actuary would have to certify that the plan had re-attained funded status before new benefit accruals could begin. As introduced, these restrictions would have applied to plans that were under-funded after credit balances had been deducted from plan assets. As amended by the Committee, the benefit restrictions would not apply if the plan's assets were at least 100% of plan liabilities *before* subtracting credit balances. In pension plans considered to be at risk of default, assets set aside in trust funds to pre-fund deferred compensation for highly compensated employees would be taxable as employee income.

PROHIBITION ON "SHUT-DOWN" BENEFITS

"Shutdown benefits" are pension payments made to long-service employees when a plant is shut down. These benefits typically are negotiated between employers and labor unions. Shutdown benefits usually are not pre-funded because the probability of future plant shutdowns is unpredictable. Because they are unfunded, shutdown benefits weaken the financial status of the PBGC when it takes over an under-funded pension plan of a company that has promised its workers these benefits. H.R. 2830 would prohibit shut-down benefits and similar "contingent-event" benefits. This change generally would be effective in 2007.[4]

DISCLOSURE REQUIREMENTS

The bill would plan administrators to provide an annual "funding notice" within 90 days of the close of the plan year to each participant and beneficiary and to any labor organization representing participants. The notice must include (1) identifying information; (2) the ratio of active to inactive participants; (3) the plan's assets and liabilities and the ratio of assets to liabilities; and (4) the plan's funding and asset allocation policies. Plan sponsors also would have to include more information on the Form 5500 that they file annually with the Internal Revenue Service, including an explanation of the actuarial assumptions used to project future retirements and asset allocations. Plans would have to provide participants a copy of the summary annual report (SAR) within 15 days of the deadline for filing the Form 5500.

Section 4010 of ERISA provides that plans underfunded by $50 million or more must file a report with the PBGC, but it prohibits the PBGC from releasing this information to the plan participants or the public. H.R. 2830 would require the plan sponsor to provide participants with a notice of their filing with the PBGC. The notice would include (1) the number of the sponsor's at-risk plans in which the ratio of assets to liabilities in the preceding plan year was less than 60%; (2) the value of the assets, the funding target, and the asset/liability ratio for each plan; and (3) the aggregate value of plan assets, plan funding targets (taking into account only vested benefits) and asset/liability ratios for all plans. The notice would have to be sent to participants no later than 90 days after the related notice is sent to PBGC. The PBGC notice is due 105 days after the close of the year. The disclosure requirements would be triggered if the plan were underfunded by $50 million or more; if the plan were less than 60% funded; or if the plan were less than 75% funded and sponsored by an employer in a financially troubled industry. Congress would also have to be given the same information sent to the PBGC.

RULES FOR MULTIEMPLOYER PLANS [5]

H.R. 2830 would establish new funding standards for multiemployer plans, with special rules for plans that are less than 80% funded. Multiemployer plan sponsors would have to amortize unfunded prior service liability over 15 years, rather than over 30 years as under current law. "Endangered" plans - those that are less than 80% funded - generally would be required to develop a plan to increase contributions, reduce or cease new benefit accruals, and adopt other plan amendments that can reasonably be expected to meet prescribed improvements in the plan's funded status within 10 years. Alternative schedules for improving solvency would apply to endangered plans that are less than 70% funded and to plans more than 70% funded but less than 80% funded. Employers currently contributing to severely underfundfed plans would be required to make 5% to 10% surcharge contributions until the next collective bargaining agreement is adopted.

Multiemployer plans would be required to furnish actuarial and financial reports within 30 days of a request from a contributing employer or labor organization, and they would have to report the amount of an employer's withdrawal liability within 180 days of receiving a written request from a contributing employer. They also would have to identify the number of contributing employers and the number of workers for whom there is no contributing employer. The bill would increase the maximum tax-deductible contribution for multiemployer plans to 140% of current liability.

INVESTMENT ADVICE

H.R. 2830 would allow advisors or affiliates of investment funds offered in a §401(k) plan to offer investment advice to plan participants. Eligible plans would be exempted from certain rules governing prohibited transactions under ERISA and the Internal Revenue Code. To qualify for this exemption, the adviser would have to meet disclosure and qualification requirements. The adviser would have to provide notice of fees, material affiliations, any limitation on the scope of advice, and services provided with respect to the advice. The notice would have to state that the adviser is acting as a fiduciary and that the participant or beneficiary could arrange for outside "third-party"advice. By providing investment advice, the adviser would be acting as a fiduciary subject to the terms of ERISA that apply to plan fiduciaries. In addition, the advisor would have to be either a registered investment adviser under the Investment Advisers Act; a bank or similar financial institution; an insurance company; a registered broker or dealer; or an affiliate, agent, or employee of one of these institutions. Fees paid to the adviser would have to be reasonable and at least as favorable as an arm's length transaction, and the participant would have to make the actual investment and asset allocation decisions. The bill defines the scope of a plan sponsor's fiduciary obligations as limited to "the prudent selection and periodic review" of the adviser, and provides that the sponsor has no duty to monitor specific investment advice given by the adviser, and therefore would not be liable for the specific advice given.

CASH BALANCE PLANS AND OTHER HYBRID PENSIONS

The Committee adopted an amendment that would establish principles for testing defined benefit plans for age discrimination and would clarify that "cash balance plans" do not ordinarily discriminate against older employees under federal law. It describes how cash balance plans and other "hybrid" pensions that have characteristics of both defined benefit and defined contribution plans would be tested for age discrimination, and clarifies that a defined benefit plan does not discriminate on the basis of age if a participant's entire accrued benefit, as defined under the plan's benefit formula, is no less than the accrued benefit of any worker similarly situated in every respect except for age. Pre-retirement indexing (for example, periodic adjustments that protect the economic value of the benefit against inflation prior to distribution) could be disregarded in making this determination. The amendment also provides that in the case of cash balance plans, paying a lump sum equal to the participant's account balance would be sufficient to prevent a prohibited forfeiture of an accrued benefit, provided that the plan credits interest at a rate no greater than a market rate of interest. The amendment would apply prospectively, i.e., after enactment.

REFERENCES

[1] *Defined benefit* pension plans usually pay benefits based on an employee's salary and years of service. With each year of service a worker earns a benefit equal to either a fixed dollar amount or a percentage of his or her final pay or average pay. Employers must pre-fund these benefits.

[2] A yield curve is a graph that shows interest rates on fixed income securities (bonds) plotted against the maturity date of the security. Normally, long-term bonds have higher yields than short-term bonds because both credit risk and inflation risk rise as the maturity dates extend further into the future. Consequently, the yield curve usually slopes upward from left to right.

[3] The bill would allow a plan sponsor to deduct for tax purposes a contribution equal to the greater of (1) 150% of current liability or (2) if the plan is not "at-risk," 100% of liability determined as if the plan were at-risk, plus the plan's normal cost, minus the value of plan assets.

[4] In 2004, the 6th U.S. Circuit Court of Appeals ruled that in order to protect its insurance program from the financial burden of unfunded benefits, the PBGC could set a plan termination date that would prevent the agency from being liable for shutdown benefits. In March 2005, the U.S. Supreme Court declined to hear the case, leaving the Circuit Court's decision in place.

[5] Multiemployer plans are common among workers covered by collective bargaining agreements.

In: Pensions: Reform, Protection and Health Insurance ISBN: 1-59454-704-1
Editor: Leo A. Felton, pp. 53-80   © 2006 Nova Science Publishers, Inc.

Chapter 3

HEALTH INSURANCE
COVERAGE FOR RETIREES[*]

Hinda Ripps Chaikind and Fran Larkins

SUMMARY

Many retired individuals depend on their former employer for retirement
health insurance as their sole source of coverage before reaching age 65, or
as a supplement to their Medicare coverage once reaching age 65. However,
the future of these benefits is uncertain. Burdened by rising costs, some
employers have already reduced or eliminated health insurance coverage for
their retirees. With the aging of the baby boom generation looming ahead,
employers offering coverage to their retired workers will face a huge future
financial commitment. For this reason, some employers are re-examining
their commitment to providing retiree health benefits to current workers.

An important feature of employer-sponsored health insurance, for
retirees and current employees, is that it is voluntary — employers are not
required to offer health insurance. There are few protections to prevent
employers from cutting or eliminating benefits, unless the employer has
made a specific promise to maintain the benefits or has a contractual
agreement with either the employee or a labor group. As a result, even
among retirees who have employer-sponsored retiree health insurance,
benefits are eroding as employers shift costs to retirees by increasing

---

[*] Excerpted from CRS Report RL32944. Updated June 9, 2005.

premiums, copayments or deductibles. For companies in bankruptcy, retiree health benefits are particularly vulnerable. Unlike defined benefit pensions that offer some protections for employees of companies in bankruptcy through the Pension Benefits Guaranty Corporation, there are no protections for retiree health benefits.

There are a wide variety of policy options currently being discussed that endeavor to make retiree coverage more available or affordable, or even to require that employers maintain coverage. However, when considering any option, it is also essential to consider the relationship between retirees' health insurance and insurance for current employees. The concept of special treatment aimed solely at protecting the retiree population, without an equivalent treatment for current employees, could lead to inequitable outcomes. Thus, any statutory requirement providing retirees with health insurance coverage should be examined in the broader context of all employer-sponsored coverage.

INTRODUCTION

Many retired individuals depend on their former employer for retirement health insurance as their sole source of coverage before reaching age 65, or as a supplement to their Medicare coverage once reaching age 65. However, given that employers are not required to offer employer-sponsored health insurance in the first place, as well as limited federal protections available for persons losing coverage, the future of these benefits is uncertain. Burdened by rising costs, some employers have already reduced or eliminated their commitment to insure their retirees. With the aging of the baby boom generation looming ahead, employers offering coverage to their retired workers will face a huge future financial commitment. Recent trends indicate that retiree health benefits are increasingly subject to higher beneficiary cost-sharing. Further, among employers who provide health insurance for current retirees, their current workers are less likely to be guaranteed these benefits upon retirement.

Retiree health insurance became prevalent after the passage of Medicare in 1965, as a result of the relatively low cost. Because Medicare is the primary payer for qualified retired beneficiaries aged 65 and older, it was fairly inexpensive for employers to provide retiree health benefits that supplemented the Medicare benefit. In the late 1980s, retiree health benefits became more expensive for employers due to both the rising costs of benefits not covered by Medicare and the changing demographics of the retiree population. For example, employer-sponsored plans often include coverage for prescription drugs, and depending on the cost-sharing arrangements and level of coverage, the cost of including prescription drug coverage can be very expensive. Retiree coverage could see further changes, once Medicare begins to cover prescription drugs in 2006. However, Medicare coverage would only affect those retirees who are over 65 and qualify for Medicare. Many individuals retire before reaching 65 and their retiree health insurance would most likely be their sole source of coverage.

Employer-sponsored retiree health insurance benefits are eroding as employers attempt to control their costs by tightening eligibility requirements and shifting costs to retirees through increased retiree premium contributions, deductibles, and copayment amounts. In some cases when employers attempt to scale back or eliminate coverage, employees have turned to the courts to try to retain their coverage. The courts have sided with retirees in only limited instances because minimal federal protections exist for retirees when employers decide to change their health insurance coverage.

DEMOGRAPHICS OF THE RETIREE POPULATION

Understanding the demographics of the retiree population helps to explain their high health insurance costs. This issue is of growing concern to employers offering retiree health insurance, especially as they face the retirement of their current "baby boom generation" workers. As this group begins to consider retirement, a combination of factors — the size of the group, their increasing life expectancies and the increase in their health costs as they age — will make it financially difficult for employers to offer them retiree health insurance. Furthermore, absent retiree health insurance from a former employer, this group can also generally expect to pay higher amounts for the same or less coverage in the individual market.

In 1965 when Medicare was created, costs were relatively low for employer-based retiree health benefits and there were few retirees compared to the number of active workers. The 18.5 million persons over age 65 comprised only 9.5% of the total population.[1] Most workers waited to retire until the age of 65 when they were eligible for retirement benefits under Social Security and health insurance coverage under Medicare. At retirement, they could expect to live until 79, another 14 years.[2]

Since that time, Americans are living longer. According to the U.S. National Center for Health Statistics, in 2001, persons reaching age 65 had an average life expectancy of an additional 18.1 years. By 2002, the total number of persons over age 65 had grown to 35.6 million, or 12.3% of the total population. As more people live into old age, the age-profile of the population will continue to shift. The first wave of the baby boom generation (persons born between 1946 and 1964) reached age 55 in 2001 and are beginning to consider options for retirement. This first wave will reach age 65 in 2011. According to U.S. Census Bureau estimates for 2030, when the baby boomers are all over age 65, the total number of persons 65 and older will have more than doubled from 35.6 million to 71.5 million and will comprise 20% of the U.S. population.

As individuals reach their late 50s and 60s, they become increasingly likely to have acute and chronic health conditions such as heart disease, arthritis, and diabetes. According to the National Center for Chronic Disease Prevention and Health Promotion, approximately 80% of all persons over age 65 have at least one chronic condition and 50% have at least two. Furthermore, after adjusting for socioeconomic factors, a lack of health insurance has been linked to an increased risk of a decline in overall health among adults in late middle age.[3] These long-term illnesses have a negative effect on quality of life and can lead to severe disability.

Retirees who have a greater prevalence of health problems are less able than workers to obtain affordable health insurance should they lose their employer-sponsored insurance before they are eligible for Medicare. Health insurance coverage is thus a major consideration for persons making the decision about whether or not to retire.

Today's workers face many choices regarding retirement age. Some employees retire as early as age 55, the minimum retirement age allowed by most defined benefit pension plans. Others don't retire until they are 62, the earliest retirement age at which Social Security benefits are first payable, though these are permanently reduced. Fewer workers wait until they reach the "full retirement age" under Social Security which in 2004 is 65 years and four months. (The age at which unreduced Social Security benefits are first payable will gradually rise to age 67.) In 2003, more than 72% of retired-worker beneficiaries had elected to receive Social Security retirement benefits before age 65.[4] Because availability of health insurance benefits is an important consideration for older workers, still others wait until the Medicare eligibility age of 65 to retire. According to Mercer, in its 2003 Survey Report-National Survey of Employee Sponsored Health Insurance, the median retirement age is 61 in organizations offering retiree health insurance compared to 63 in those that do not.

Because Americans approaching or at retirement age consume more medical services than younger persons, their health care is more expensive. According to the U.S. Administration on Aging's report, *A Profile of Older Americans: 2003*, the elderly averaged $3,586 in out-of-pocket health care expenditures in 2002. This can be compared to the average out-of-pocket costs for the total population of only $2,350. Even when near-elderly workers (ages 55 to 64) with health problems are insured and have access to needed health services, they have average annual expenditures of $5,000, nearly twice the level of their counterparts in excellent or very good health ($2,548).[5] Employment-based insurance spreads these costs over all its enrollees in the same plan, but private non-group insurance premiums generally reflect the higher risk attributable to the policyholder's age and health status. A 2001 Commonwealth Fund study found that adults aged 50 to 64 who buy individual coverage are likely to pay much more out-of-pocket for a limited package of benefits than their counterparts who are covered by their employers. An analysis of premium costs for individual coverage in 15 cities showed a median cost of nearly $6,000 for individual coverage for a 60-year-old. Group rates would have been less than half this amount, with a median annual premium cost of employer insurance of $2,520 for a preferred provider organization (PPO) plan, and workers would have been required to pay only 14% of this amount for single coverage.[6]

HEALTH INSURANCE COVERAGE

Retirees with Employer-Sponsored Health Insurance

Retirees from large firms are more likely to be offered health insurance than workers retiring from smaller firms. In fact, the prevalence of retiree coverage increases with firm size. For example, employees under age 65 retiring from firms with 20,000 or more employees are twice as likely to be offered coverage as employees in firms of 500-999 employees. Retirees over age 65 are almost three times as likely to be offered retiree health benefits in the largest firms.[7]

However, regardless of firm size, the percentage of employers offering retiree coverage has been steadily declining over the last decade. The percentage of firms with more than 200 workers that offer retiree coverage fell by almost half between 1988 and 2004, from 66% to 36%.[8] In 1993, 46% of employers with at least 500 employees offered coverage to their pre-Medicare eligibles and by 2003 this figure declined to 28% of employers.

Similarly, 40% of employers with at least 500 employees offered coverage to their Medicare eligibles in 1993, compared to 21% in 2003.[9] As shown in **Table 1**, there has been a steady decline in coverage over the period.

**Table 1. Percentage of Large Firms Offering
Retiree Health Coverage, 1993-2003**

Year	Pre-Medicare eligible retirees	Medicare eligible retirees
1993	46%	40%
1995	41%	35%
1997	38%	31%
1999	35%	28%
2001	29%	23%
2003	28%	21%

Source: National Survey of Employer Sponsored Health Plans, 2003 Survey Report, Mercer.

Other Sources of Insurance for Retirees

Sources of health insurance are very different for those individuals under age 65 than for those who are over 65 and most likely covered by Medicare. However, according to CRS calculations of Medicare Current Beneficiary Survey Data for 2002, Medicare only covers about half of the medical costs of the 65 and older group.[10] To help defray costs of services not covered by Medicare, most Medicare beneficiaries have additional health insurance coverage, including employee coverage, government coverage, and private supplementary coverage obtained through an individually purchased policy, commonly referred to as Medigap. In 2002, less than 8% of Medicare beneficiaries had no additional coverage, as shown in **Figure 1**. Almost another 12% of Medicare eligibles enrolled in a Medicare managed care plan (Medicare Advantage),[11] which while not technically "additional insurance", does in many cases provide extra services beyond the basic package of Medicare benefits.

For retirees who are under age 65, and do not qualify for Medicare based on disability or End-Stage Renal Disease (ESRD),[12] insurance options are more limited. Absent retiree health insurance, insurance through a spouse, or access to Medicaid or other federal programs, these retirees would have to purchase insurance in the individual market if they chose to be covered. Retirees moving from their employer's group plan to an individually purchased product are provided with certain guarantees for health insurance coverage under federal law. However, while federal law guarantees the availability of health insurance for these individuals moving from the group to the individual market,[13] there are no federal limits on the premium amounts that may be charged. Because individual policies are likely to be subject to underwriting (based on information such as the individual's age and medical history) premiums would also likely be higher, particularly for older and sicker individuals. Some states have passed laws to limit premium amounts, providing varying degrees of protection.

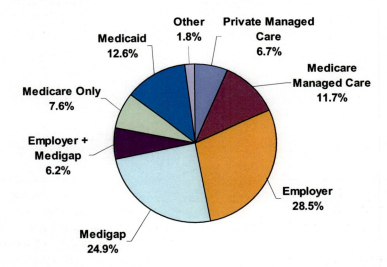

Figure 1. Supplemental Insurance Categories for the Medicare Non-Institutionalized Population, 2002

Erosion in Coverage over Time

According to a Kaiser/Hewitt December 2004 survey of large private-sector employers, between 2003 and 2004, 79% of large companies surveyed had increased the share of the premiums paid by the retiree, 53% indicated that they had increased the amount enrollees pay for prescription drugs, 45% had increased cost-sharing requirements for other services, and 8% had eliminated subsidized retiree health benefits for their new employees.[14]

Employers are also managing their retiree health insurance costs by providing different benefits for current and future retirees. For example, some employers who offer retiree health insurance to their current retirees will not provide coverage for individuals who retire in the future. Other firms may only provide group access to health insurance for future retirees, requiring them to pay 100% of the premiums. Firms may also use a sliding scale based on factors such as age at retirement, years of service at retirement, or a combination of the two to determine their premium contributions for retirees. According to the 2003 Mercer National Survey of Employer-Sponsored Health Plans, 30% of firms offering retiree health based their share of premium contributions on age and years of service. Among large employers (500 or more employees), about 38% of pre-Medicare retirees pay 100% of their premium, 49% share the premium costs with the employer, and 13% have their total premium paid for by the employer. For the Medicare-aged retirees, 37% pay 100% of their premium, 47% share the costs with the employer and 15% have the total premium paid by the employer.

Role of the Law and Courts

An important feature about employer-sponsored health insurance, for both retirees and current employees, is that employers are not required to offer health insurance. There are few protections to prevent employers from cutting or eliminating benefits, unless the employer has made a specific promise to maintain the benefits or has a contractual agreement with either the employee or a labor group. Employers or other plan sponsors are generally free to adopt, modify, or terminate "welfare benefits," which includes health insurance, as long as they have preserved their right to modify such plans. Therefore, the documents governing the plan are crucial. According to Employee Retirement Income Security Act of 1974 (ERISA, P.L. 93-406) requirements, employers are required to provide individuals with a copy of the summary plan description (SPD) within 90 days after they become a plan participant. The SPD can change each year, but the SPD in effect when the individual retired may be the controlling document. Employers may explicitly reserve the right in the SPD and in other documents to change the terms of the plan. Additionally, even when these documents promise that health benefits will continue, they may not rule out the possibility for changes such as reduced benefits or increased copayments. Language in the plan may be vague and as a result the courts have been asked to step in to settle disputes. Records, correspondence, brochures, or other documents that contain information about the duration or scope of coverage may be used for clarification, as well as labor agreements that provide documentation clarifying retiree coverage.

As a result of limited if any protections, retirees have turned to the courts to seek relief. However, in cases in which the employer has maintained the right to modify or terminate a plan, the courts have sided with the employers (e.g., *Curtiss-Wright Corp. v. Schoonejongen)*[15] In other instances, when employers have not preserved their right to change a plan (e.g., *Eardman v. Bethlehem Steel*),[16] the courts have sided with the employee.[17]

Another issue brought before the courts was whether or not employers could offer health benefits to their Medicare-eligible retirees that differed from those offered to their retirees who were not Medicare eligible. In *Erie County Retirees Association v. County of Erie, Pennsylvania*, a 2000 case involving a group of Medicare-eligible retirees and the Age Discrimination and Employment Act (ADEA), the U.S. Court of Appeals for the Third Circuit found that the county had distinguished impermissibly between its Medicare-eligible retirees and its younger retirees with respect to their health insurance coverage based on the age of the retirees.[18] Despite the apparent violation, the case was remanded to determine whether the county's actions were protected by the ADEA so-called equal benefit safe harbor provisions.[19] Later a settlement was reached between the county and the Medicare-eligible retirees. Along this line, the Equal Employment Opportunity Commission (EEOC) issued a proposed exception to ADEA allowing employers to alter, reduce, or eliminate retiree health benefits when retirees become eligible for Medicare. The EEOC was planning to release a final rule, when the American Association of Retired Persons was granted a preliminary injunction on the regulation. On March 30, 2005 a federal district judge blocked the rule, issuing a permanent injunction to prohibit federal officials from publishing or implementing the regulation. EEOC reportedly plans to appeal the ruling to the Third Circuit. If issued as a final regulation, employers would be allowed to segment their retiree population, providing different retiree coverage for those over 65 than for those under 65. This could become even more significant once the new Medicare prescription drug program begins in 2006. For example, plans could eliminate their prescription drug coverage for their Medicare eligible retirees, requiring these individuals to enroll in Medicare Part D if they wanted to continue to receive prescription drug coverage. However, the standard Medicare Part D prescription drug benefit is generally less generous than coverage offered by employers.

REASONS FOR ERODING COVERAGE AND ISSUES

The erosion of health insurance coverage for the retiree population is based on several factors. As previously discussed, the demographics of this group foreshadow that employers may be facing coverage for a larger number of individuals who are expected to live longer and therefore use a lot more health care services than originally anticipated when these companies first began to offer retiree health coverage. In addition, several other factors, described below, contribute to the erosion of retiree health insurance, including increasing costs, especially for prescription drugs, the economy, and changes in accounting practices.

Costs of Health Insurance

According to the Kaiser/Hewitt January 2004 survey, among their 333 surveyed employers with more than 1,000 employees, total costs for employer-sponsored retiree coverage were $18.1 billion in 2002, including costs paid by the retiree and the employer. This figure increased by 13.7%, growing to an estimated $20.6 billion in 2003.[20]

The cost to employers for providing these benefits has been increasing, due to an increasing number of retirees, as well as increased per capita costs. According to Mercer, between 2002 and 2003, retiree medical costs for pre-Medicare eligibles increased by 14% (with premiums increasing from $6,956 to $7,948) and by 11% (with premiums increasing from $2,702 to $3,003) for Medicare eligible retirees.[21]

Looking at an overall premium increase for employer-sponsored health insurance (not solely premium increases for retiree health insurance), according to the Kaiser/HRET 2004 annual survey, increases in health insurance premiums are outpacing increases in both workers' earning and overall inflation. For example, premiums increased by 11.2% from 2003 to 2004, compared with a 2.2% increase in earnings and a 2.3% increase in inflation.[22] In the early 1990s premium increases were smaller each year, bottoming out at less than a 1% increase in 1996. However, increases have gotten progressively larger since then, reaching double digits in 2001. There was a slowdown in the increase between 2003 and 2004 from 13.9% to 11.2%, although still a double digit increase. Double digit increases in premiums are expected to continue, in part due to the anticipated continuation of the upwards turn in the underwriting cycle, and in part due to increasing costs (inflation and utilization) of medical claims.[23] The largest of these increases appear to be concentrated in the smallest firms.

Prescription Drug Coverage

While most firms providing retiree coverage offer prescription drug coverage, it is more prevalent for larger firms. On average, 94% of these large employers (at least 500 employees) offering retiree coverage include prescription drug coverage. Among firms with 500-999 workers, 92% offer coverage, increasing to 98% for firms with more than 20,000 employers.[24]

The annual increase in prescription drug spending has outpaced that of overall medical benefits, in large part because of increased prescription drug utilization. As a result, employers have looked for ways to hold down their costs for providing prescription drug coverage, by ratcheting down these benefits. Plans have continued to develop cost-saving mechanisms, such as increasing cost-sharing or requiring a mail-order prescription refill. Plans are also increasingly using three-tier payment arrangements, such as one tier with lower out-of-pocket costs for the enrollee purchasing generic drugs, and two tiers for non-generic drugs (preferred and non-preferred).

Beginning in 2006, Medicare beneficiaries will be offered a new voluntary benefit providing prescription drug coverage, as established in the Medicare Prescription Drug, Improvement, and Modernization Act of 2003, P.L. 108-173. Medicare beneficiaries will be able to purchase either "standard coverage" or alternative coverage with at least actuarially equivalent benefits. In 2006, "standard coverage" will have a $250 deductible, 25% coinsurance for approved drug costs between $251 and $2,250, then no coverage until the beneficiary has out-of-pocket costs of $3,600 ($5,100 in total spending). Once the beneficiary reaches the catastrophic limit, the beneficiary will pay nominal cost sharing. Coverage can be provided through prescription drug plans or through a Medicare Advantage plan for individuals enrolled in such a plan offering prescription drug coverage.

Once Medicare begins to cover prescription drugs, employers may decide to make changes to their health plans for retirees with respect to prescription drug coverage, or even to their entire benefit package. Employers who continue to provide retiree prescription drug coverage that is actuarially equivalent to or better than Medicare coverage may be eligible for a federal subsidy, as long as the retiree is eligible for but does not sign up for the Medicare prescription drug benefit. Subsidy payments will equal 28% of a retiree's gross[25] covered retiree plan-related prescription drug costs over the $250 deductible up to $5,000. (The dollar amounts would be adjusted annually by the percentage increase in Medicare per capita prescription drug costs.)

In the Kaiser/Hewitt December 2004 survey, the majority of responding employers indicated that they were likely to continue to offer prescription drug coverage, even after Medicare coverage begins. However, once the program is in place, employers may wish to reassess their decision as to whether or not to continue retiree coverage for either the entire retiree heath package or just the prescription drug coverage. For example, if the subsidy covers a significant portion of the employer's cost for providing prescription drug coverage, then the employer's continued coverage might be a financially viable option. On the other hand, some employers may no longer be willing to provide either prescription drug or even any retiree coverage, once Medicare prescription drug coverage is available. Some employers may only have been willing to provide retiree coverage in the past because it was generally a retiree's sole source for prescription drug coverage. With the inclusion of some coverage under Medicare, even if it is more limited than the employer's coverage, an employer may no longer feel a responsibility to provide coverage to its retirees. Employers could drop the drug coverage or even choose to drop all health insurance for retirees. The employer does have the option of discontinuing its prescription drug coverage and paying the Medicare prescription drug premium for its employees.

Finally, younger retirees, those under 65, will still depend on their employers for prescription drug coverage. If the EEOC eventually issues its proposed exception to ADEA, then employers could provide prescription drug benefits for only their younger retirees and not their Medicare eligible retirees.

Financial Downturn

During the booming economic years of the late 1990s, some employees were shielded from the increasing health insurance costs. Firms were willing to absorb these costs in order to remain competitive in a tight labor market. However, as costs continued to escalate, and the economy took a downward turn employers found themselves less able to absorb these costs. Furthermore, as the job market weakened and workers had a more difficult time finding or switching jobs, employers did not need to provide as many incentives to attract employees, and thus were less likely or willing to absorb increasing health insurance costs. This issue is especially critical for small firms, who often operate on narrow margins with little room to absorb increased costs. Not surprisingly, the decline in offering health insurance coverage is most notable among these small firms.

Accounting Rules (FASB and GASB)

Effective for fiscal years beginning after December 15, 1992, the Financial Accounting Standards Board (FASB) established new requirements for the reporting of non-pension retiree benefits in FAS 106, which includes health benefits. This rule significantly changed the practice of pay-as-you-go accounting for these post-retirement benefits to accrual accounting. The employer's expense for these benefits is now incurred at the time the employee renders the services necessary to earn their post-retirement benefits, that is the employer must account for the cost of retiree health insurance while the employee is working for the firm, rather than waiting until the employee retires and enrolls in the retiree health insurance plan. This accounting standard requires companies to more closely examine health insurance costs for their retirees and this examination may have led them to realize the magnitude of these costs.

In response to FAS 106, some companies announced changes in benefit programs, such as eliminating retiree health coverage, establishing caps on their dollar contribution, increasing cost-sharing, and linking the level of benefits with the years of service. FAS 106 may have provided a convenient rationale for reducing or eliminating retiree coverage. It may have also made some employers realize that their commitment to retiree health insurance was open-ended and growing at a rapid pace.

Establishing caps, as a practical matter, limits the open-ended nature of a firm's liability, and thus constrains the dollar amounts that they would have to recognize as a result of the FAS 106 rules. Firms often set the caps at a level they expected to reach at some future date, possibly even 10-20 years in the future. However, given the rapid rate of increase in health insurance costs, employers may find that they exceed the cap even sooner than anticipated, presenting an interesting dilemma for the provision of retiree health benefits. First, firms could raise the caps; however, this would require higher spending.[26] Alternatively, they could choose to adhere to the caps, thus eroding retiree health insurance, by either increasing the retiree's contribution, or reducing benefits.

Another potential issue is the convergence of the cap and the employer's subsidy for actuarially equivalent prescription drug benefits under Medicare. Some firms may initially meet the standards required for receiving the subsidy in 2006. Over time, as the cost of insurance increases, some firms will reach and exceed their cap, thus possibly facing a problem, because once the cap is exceeded, the value of their benefits would decline. As a result, employers who at one time met the actuarial equivalent standard required under Medicare law, may no longer meet that standard. Then they may no longer qualify for the 28% employer subsidy.[27]

On the other hand, when companies reduce their retirees' health benefits, they are not only spending less for these benefits, they are also able to report smaller post-retirement health costs. For example, in response to Medicare prescription drug coverage in 2006, some companies are planning to maintain their prescription drug coverage and will receive a 28% subsidy, which would reduce their post-retirement health costs. Other companies may reduce their health plan costs, by eliminating or reducing prescription drug coverage, which would also reduce their liability.

Recently, the Government Accounting Standards Board (GASB) adopted statement No. 43, which changed the accounting rules for the costs of various post-employment benefits for state and local governments. The new standard is similar to FAS 106 standards in that it requires accrual accounting, but provides greater flexibility. For example, FAS 106 prescribes a single actuarial method for the calculation of post-retirement health costs, while GASB 43 allows a choice between several different actuarial methods. The application of GASB 43 could have a similar impact on employers' commitment, causing them to rethink their retirees' health insurance coverage. However, because this group of employees is state and local government workers, they may have more bargaining power, or union protections, than some of the groups in the private sector that were affected by FAS 106.

POLICY OPTIONS

Out of concern for maintaining health insurance coverage for retirees, legislative proposals have been offered to provide them some protections. There are a wide variety of policy options currently being discussed that endeavor to make retiree coverage more available or affordable, or even to require that employers maintain coverage. However, when considering any option, it is also essential to consider the relationship between retirees' health insurance and insurance for current employees. Special treatment for retirees, compared to current workers could lead to inequitable outcomes. For example, one policy option often discussed to protect retiree health insurance is to require employers to continue to provide previously promised health insurance coverage to their retiree population. Without a parallel requirement for current workers, employers could find themselves in a situation where they were financially unable to cover workers, but required to cover retirees. Thus any statutory requirement to provide retiree health insurance coverage should be examined in the broader context of all employer-sponsored coverage.

Modify COBRA

Under Title X of the Consolidated Omnibus Budget Reconciliation Act of 1985 (COBRA, P.L. 99-272), an employer with 20 or more employees must provide employees and their families with the option to continue their coverage under the employer's group health insurance plan in the case of certain events.[28] The former employee is responsible for paying the premium, which is limited to 100% of the rate charged to current employees, plus an additional 2% for administrative costs. In general, when a covered employee experiences a termination or reduction in hours of employment, including retirement, the continued coverage for the employee and the employee's spouse and dependent children must be offered for 18 months.

If a firm offers retiree health insurance coverage, retirees would most likely decline the temporary coverage provided under COBRA in favor of the retiree coverage, which may be less expensive (if the employer pays part of the premium) and would not be limited to only 18 months. However, if an individual chooses retiree coverage and the firm later discontinues this coverage, the retiree (no longer a current worker) would not be eligible to elect COBRA. Only those retirees who lose retiree health insurance benefits due to the bankruptcy (reorganization under Chapter 11) of their former employer may elect COBRA coverage that can continue until their death. Their spouses and dependent children may continue COBRA coverage for an additional 36 months after the death of the retiree. Furthermore, COBRA coverage is only available as long as the firm continues to offer health insurance to its current workers. As a result, when firms declare bankruptcy and cease operations, there are no current workers and no health insurance, so that the retirees (as well as displaced workers) have no health benefits available to purchase under COBRA. Unlike defined benefit pensions that offer some protections for employees of companies in bankruptcy through the Pension Benefits Guaranty Corporation, there are no protections for retiree health.

One option often discussed for providing health insurance coverage to individuals who retire before reaching age 65 (eligibility age for Medicare) is to expand COBRA by allowing younger retirees to continue to purchase their coverage through their former employer, until they reach 65. There are some advantages and disadvantages for both retirees and employers of expanding COBRA coverage. For retirees, the greatest advantage may be their ability to purchase the same coverage they were offered as employees. Although the Health Insurance Portability and Accountability Act (HIPAA, P.L. 104-191) requires that certain individuals moving from the group to individual market are guaranteed the right to purchase health insurance coverage, HIPAA does not limit premiums. Older individuals, especially those with more health care needs, may find that the available individual market coverage is very expensive. Even the COBRA premium costs (up to 102% of premiums) may be prohibitively expensive for individuals whose incomes decline once they retire, complicated by the fact that while they were working their employers most likely paid a large share of the premium. For some employers, there may be an incentive to substitute this expanded COBRA coverage for other retiree coverage, thus decreasing the share of retiree health insurance they offer. Employers, on the other hand, have argued that the 2% administrative allowance does not adequately cover their additional burden. Furthermore, individuals who choose COBRA are likely to be less healthy than the rest of the employee population, so that 102% of premiums that employers are allowed to charge could be significantly lower than the claims's incurred for the COBRA enrollees.

Tax Deductions or Credits

Under current law, the tax treatment of premiums paid by employers makes it attractive for both employers and employees to purchase employer-sponsored health insurance. Any amount that an employer pays towards premiums is not counted as taxable income for the employee and not subject to payroll taxes by both the employer and employee. Additionally, some employees are able to pay any required premium contribution from pre-tax dollars. Retirees, unlike current workers, cannot pay for their share of any premium from pre-tax dollars. For most individuals who purchase their health insurance outside of their job, the only allowable tax deduction is available to those who itemize and have health care expenditures exceeding 7.5% of adjusted gross income.

Expanding tax options, such as allowing a tax deduction for premiums paid by retirees or for those taxpayers who do not itemize, may make these premiums more affordable whether the retiree has to pay all of the premium or some lesser share. Additionally providing tax credits is another option for reducing taxes, thus making premiums more affordable. Currently, there is a tax credit available on a limited basis for a select group of individuals.[29] Credits could be expanded and designed to cover a retiree's entire share of premiums, could be limited to a specific dollar amount, could be linked to income or any combination of the three. However, establishing tax credits for health insurance raises complex issues. One important question is whether the credit would be the same for all taxpayers or more generous for those with lower incomes. The credits would need to be large enough to encourage individuals to buy the insurance, but might also have the adverse effect of providing employers with an incentive to reduce their commitment to health insurance. Additionally, if individuals with tax credits did not have access to the group market, they might have limited and/or only expensive options for buying health insurance, thus limiting the buying power of the credit.

Tax-Advantaged Accounts for Health Care Expenditures

There are a number of tax-advantaged accounts permitted under current law that can be used for unreimbursed qualified medical expenses such as deductibles, copayments and services not covered by health insurance.[30] The newest of these types of accounts is the Health Savings Account (HSA) established in the Medicare Prescription Drug, Improvement, and Modernization Act of 2003, (P.L. 108-173). HSAs are personal savings accounts for qualified medical expenses not covered by insurance or otherwise reimbursable. They can be established and contributions made only when the account owners are covered by a qualifying high deductible insurance plan and have no other coverage, with some exceptions. Annual contributions to HSAs are limited to the lesser of the deductible or a federally established limit. Additional "catch-up" contributions (limited to $600 in 2005 and reaching $1,000 by 2009) are allowed for individuals who are at least 55 years of age but not enrolled in Medicare. Unused portions of HSAs may be carried over from one year to the next, so that even though Medicare-enrolled individuals are not allowed to add money to an HSA account, they may continue to use any accumulated funds indefinitely. The HSA may be used to pay for the plan's cost sharing, long-term care insurance premiums, COBRA premiums, Medicare Part B premiums, and other qualified medical expenses as defined by the Internal Revenue Service. HSA funds may also be used for non-medical expenditures, subject to income tax and, for those under 65, a penalty.

Thus any unused accumulated HSA funds may be very beneficial for retirees. If the rules for contributing to HSAs were expanded, these funds have the potential of being even more useful, although opponents of HSAs already are concerned with their potential for syphoning off the healthier population and increasing insurance costs for people with the highest healthcare needs. Expanding opportunities to contribute to these funds could exacerbate these problems. While these issues must be considered, HSAs have the potential to be altered and expanded for individuals to help them pay for their own retiree health insurance coverage. For example, individuals could be allowed to contribute even higher amounts each year (over the deductible), could be allowed to make even larger contributions after reaching age 55, or even to continue making contributions after enrolling in Medicare. If individuals were allowed to put larger sums into the account for medical expenses, then the structure of the fund might need to be changed, so that withdrawals could only be used for medical expenses.

As an example, the Employee Benefit Research Institute (EBRI) calculated contributions to an HSA for 10, 20, or 30 years, along with the allowed catch-up payments for individuals over 55 years old. They assumed that the funds in the HSA would earn 5% interest and that individuals would be allowed to contribute the maximum of $2,600 per year, indexed for inflation. They did not assume that any withdrawals would be made for medical or other expenditures, although some or all of these funds would almost certainly be withdrawn over the years. In their example, a 55-year old individual contributing $2,600 (an estimate of the allowed contribution in a given year), plus catch up payments, earning 5% on funds held in the HSA, with the maximum allowable contribution indexed for inflation, could accumulate a maximum of $44,000 by age 65. If the individual were allowed to contribute for 20 years, the fund would grow to $101,000 and after 30 years it would grow to $190,000.[31] These figures only represent the contributions and earned interest, but no withdrawals.

Another tax-advantaged account is a Flexible Spending Account (FSA). Contributions to an FSA are voluntary, with accounts usually funded by an employee (although employers aren't prohibited from contributing) from his or her pre-taxed salary, thereby reducing taxable income. Funds in a Health

Care FSA (HCFSA) can be used to pay for qualified medical expenses that are not reimbursed or covered by any other source. Qualified medical expenses include coinsurance amounts, copayments, deductibles, dental care, glasses, hearing aids, as well as certain over-the-counter medical supplies that are not cosmetic in nature. One significant limitation of the HCFSA is that funds cannot be carried over from one year to the next so that unused funds are forfeited at the end of the year.[32] Another limitation is that only current employees and not annuitants are eligible to contribute to an FSA on a pre-tax basis.[33] Allowing these funds to be carried over from year to year and accumulate, allowing retirees to also contribute to FSAs on a pre-tax basis, or allowing FSA funds to be used for premiums of retirees, are all options that could help retirees pay for their own health insurance.

Similar to expanding these funds, proposals have been discussed that would allow withdrawals above the current limit from other tax-favored accounts for retirement savings, such as IRAs and 401(k) plans, as long as the withdrawals were for medical expenses.

Medicare Buy-in

Most persons age 65 and older, and certain disabled individuals, are automatically entitled to Medicare Part A, Hospital Insurance. These individuals, or their spouses, established entitlement by paying the HI payroll tax on earnings for the required number of quarters of Medicare-covered employment. Enrollment in Medicare Part B, Supplementary Medicare Insurance (SMI), and Medicare Part D, prescription drug coverage (available in 2006), are voluntary and qualified individuals choosing to enroll are required to pay a monthly premium.

One option for increasing coverage for the younger retirees is to allow individuals to purchase Medicare, prior to their attaining age 65. However, similar to COBRA coverage, the premiums could be prohibitive, and as a result several options for lowering premiums have been discussed. For example, one option would be to spread out the premiums over time, so that the premium charged to an individual under age 65 would cover only part of the costs. Once attaining Medicare eligibility, the individual would pay the standard Medicare Part B premium plus an additional monthly amount for the rest of his or her life, to compensate for the costs of the earlier care. A similar arrangement could be developed for the prescription drug benefit, Part D of Medicare. Initially the total program costs would be higher than revenues, but as the population aged, revenues from the older individuals paying the incremental premium amount would offset the unmet expenses of the younger group.

Federal Employee's Health Benefits Program Buy-in

Federal employees, Members of Congress, annuitants, and qualified dependents are entitled to participate in the Federal Employee's Health Benefits program (FEHBP). FEHBP is the largest employer-sponsored health insurance program, covering about 8.2 million individuals. FEHBP offers enrollees a choice of nationally available fee-for-service plans, HMOs serving limited geographic areas, as well as high deductible health plans coupled with tax advantaged accounts (e.g., HSAs). The government's share of premiums, which is the same for workers as it is for retirees, is 72% of the weighted average premium of all plans in the program, not to exceed 75% of any given plan's premium. Although there is no core or standard benefit package required for FEHBP plans, all plans cover basic hospital, surgical, physician, and emergency care. Plans are required to cover certain special benefits including prescription drugs (which may have separate deductibles and coinsurance); mental health care with parity of coverage relative to general medical care coverage; child immunizations; and protection of enrollee out-of-pocket costs for "catastrophic" health care costs.

Similar to the Medicare buy-in, Congress has considered proposals to allow small businesses and individuals, whether they are working or retired, to buy into FEHBP. Some of these proposals would require that plans choosing to participate in FEHBP would also be required to make these same plans available to the newly qualifying group of individuals or businesses. Most often these proposals separate the risk pools for the newly qualifying eligibles from the currently existing pool of eligibles. In this case, premiums for the new group could potentially be higher than premiums for the existing federal pool, because the new pool wouldn't have the advantage of spreading the risk across 8.2 million people. As a result, premiums for the expanded FEHBP might not be significantly less expensive than other individual or small group options available in the market today. On the other hand, if risk was spread across the entire group of new enrollees, essentially developing a new large group entity, then premiums could be less than these entities could find on their own. The key advantage of the expanded FEHBP might be that it offered this new group availability, choice and a guarantee that the products being purchased (the same offered to federal employees, annuitants and Members of Congress) included a reasonable set of benefits.

Enhance Medicare

Medicare is the primary payer for qualifying retirees over age 65. If a retired Medicare enrollee also has employer-sponsored retiree health insurance coverage, that insurance would "wrap around" the Medicare benefit paying for coinsurance, deductibles, and services covered by the plan but not Medicare. Expanding Medicare might replace or reduce the costs of retiree health insurance for this population. Although employers cannot divide their retiree population into Medicare and non-Medicare retiree groups, more Medicare coverage translates into overall reduced costs for employer's covering retirees, as this coverage would be secondary to Medicare for the Medicare eligible group. As previously mentioned, Medicare covers only about one-half of a beneficiary's average medical expenses. This percentage may increase, with the expansion of Medicare to include prescription drug coverage, beginning in 2006. However, even for retirees covered by Medicare, there are services that Medicare does not cover, such as long-term care expenses. Also, Medicare does not have a catastrophic limit on beneficiary out-of-pocket expenditures for covered services, (with the exception of Part D prescription drug services and regional Medicare managed care plans, beginning in 2006). Medicare could be enhanced to expand coverage or to offer a catastrophic limit. However, as Medicare will begin to offer a new costly prescription drug benefit in 2006, it is unlikely that other large expansions will take place in the near future that might serve to replace or reduce the costs of retiree health insurance.

Employer Mandates

Employer-sponsored health insurance is offered voluntarily by employers and in general,[34] they have the right to change coverage at any time. This includes changes such as raising copayments, increasing deductibles, requiring larger premium contributions from employees, using formularies for prescription drug coverage, or even eliminating coverage entirely. Employer mandates could be established to require that any retiree coverage offered to either current retirees and/or promised to current workers upon retirement could not be changed or eliminated. However, employers who wanted to reduce their health insurance costs, and were not allowed to change the coverage for their retirees would be forced to reduce costs only for their workers. In this situation, the retiree coverage would not change while the worker's would, possibly resulting in more generous benefits for retirees than workers. Although rather unlikely, in the most extreme case, employers could drop coverage for workers, while still providing coverage for retirees. The more likely outcome of a such a requirement is that employers could reduce benefits, increase premium contributions, deductibles, or coinsurance for current workers, while still being required to maintain the more generous package for their retired workers. Furthermore, faced with restrictions, employers might discontinue offering the promise of retiree health benefits to newly hired individuals, so that at least for this group of employees, they would not be required to offer retiree benefits when these workers eventually retire.

Pre-funding Retiree Health Benefits

Unlike defined benefit pension plans, there is no requirement that employers pre-fund their retiree health benefit plans. The ideal pre-funding vehicle would allow employers to take a tax deduction for contributions to the fund, permit sufficient amounts to be contributed for orderly accumulation of funds to discharge future obligations, and allow for investment income on the fund to be tax-free. These are all advantages enjoyed by defined benefit pension trusts.

Under current law, such an ideal funding vehicle is only available for certain employee populations. Specifically, an employer sponsoring a retiree health plan for a collectively bargained employee population may set up a Voluntary Employee Beneficiary Association (VEBA) to pre-fund retiree health benefits for this population. Such a VEBA has comparable advantages to a defined benefit pension trust. Investment income on a VEBA established to pre-fund retiree health benefits for non-union employees, on the other hand, is subject to the unrelated business income tax. Moreover, health care inflation may not be taken into account in determining the contribution to such a VEBA. Some employers have used a 401(h) sub-account of a defined benefit pension plan for the pre-funding of retiree health benefits. While the investment income on assets in such a sub-account is tax-free, only limited amounts can be contributed to it. To date, employers who have pre-funded retiree health plans have tended to be utilities such as gas and electric companies who could include the cost of pre-funding in rates charged to consumers.

LEGISLATIVE PROPOSALS

Bills that address retirees' health insurance coverage are included in the discussion below. These include legislation that has been introduced in the 109th Congress. This list may not include all relevant bills. These bills cover a wide variety of options for making retiree coverage more available and affordable such as, options to expand Medicare or FEHBP coverage to certain retirees, prohibit group plans from reducing benefits for retirees, or provide tax relief. Several bills address the needs of specific groups of retirees. Other legislation provides for comprehensive health insurance for all Americans, not just retirees.

Expand Medicare or FEHBP Coverage

- **H.R. 55** would make FEHBP available to individuals age 55 to 65 who would not otherwise have health insurance.
- **H.R. 2072** would provide access to Medicare benefits for individuals ages 55 to 65 and would amend the Internal Revenue Code of 1986 to allow a refundable and advanceable credit against income tax for payment of such premiums.

Protect Retirees Who Lose Their Health Coverage

- **S. 329** would increase the amount of unsecured claims for salaries and wages given priority in bankruptcy to provide for cash payment to retirees to compensate for lost health insurance benefits resulting from bankruptcy of their former employer.
- **H.R. 1322** would prohibit profitable employers from making any changes to retiree health benefits once an employee retired. The bill would require plan sponsors to restore benefits for retirees whose health coverage was reduced before enactment of the bill, and create a loan guarantee program to help firms restore benefits. It would not restrict employers from changing retiree health benefits for current employees.

Provide Tax Relief

- **H.R. 218** would allow a deduction for amounts paid for health insurance and prescription drug costs of individuals.
- **H.R. 2176** would provide a 100 percent deduction for the health insurance costs of individuals.
- **H.R. 2089, H.R. 765, and S. 160** would allow individuals a refundable credit against income tax for the purchase of private health insurance, subject to income and other limitations.
- **H.R. 1872 and S. 978** would provide tax incentives for the purchase of qualified health insurance.

Protect Specifically Defined Groups of Retirees Through a Variety of Methods

- **H.R. 299 and S. 162** would clarify that certain coal industry health benefits may not be modified or terminated.
- **H.R. 602 and S. 407** would restore health care coverage to certain retired members of the uniformed services.
- **H.R. 322** would allow a refundable credit to military retirees for premiums paid for coverage under Medicare Part B.
- **H.R. 994 and S. 484** would allow federal civilian and military retirees to pay health insurance premiums on a pretax basis and allowed a deduction for TRICARE supplemental premiums.

Provide Comprehensive Employer or National Health Insurance

- **H.R. 15, H.R. 676, H.R. 1200, and H.R. 2133** would establish national health insurance programs.
- **H.R. 1955, S. 637, and S. 874** would establish a national health program administered by the Office of Personnel Management to offer health benefits plans to individuals who are not federal employees.

REFERENCES

[1]   U.S. Bureau of the Census, Historical Statistics of the United States Colonial Times to 1970 Bicentennial Edition, Part 1, Series A 29-42 (Washington, DC, 1975).

[2]   William J. Wiatrowski, Retiree Health Benefits: Data Collection Issues, U.S. Department of Labor, Bureau of Labor Statistics, Compensation and Working Conditions Online, Originally posted July 29, 2003, at [http://www.bls.gov/opub/cwc/print/ cm20030711ar01ps.htm]

[3]   David W. Baker, Joseph J. Sudano, Jeffrey M. Albert, Elaine A. Borawski, and Avi Dor, "Lack of Health Insurance and Decline in Overall Health in Late Middle Age," New England Journal of Medicine, Oct. 11, 2001.

[4]   2003 Annual Statistical Supplement to the Social Security Bulletin, Social Security Administration, July 2004.

[5]   Alan C. Monheit, Jessica P. Vistnes, and John M. Eisenberg, "Moving to Medicare: Trends in the Health Insurance Status of Near-Elderly Workers, 1987-1996," Health Affairs, Mar./Apr. 2001.

[6]   Elisabeth Simantov, Cathy Schoen and Stephanie Bruegman, "Market Failure? Individual Insurance Markets for Older Americans," Health Affairs, July/Aug. 2001.

[7]   National Survey of Employer Sponsored Health Plans, 2003 Survey Tables, Mercer.

[8]   Kaiser/HRET Employer Health Benefits: 2004 Annual Survey.

[9]   National Survey of Employer Sponsored Health Plans, 2003 Survey Report, Mercer.

[10] Medicare will cover a larger share of medical costs beginning in 2006, for enrollees who purchase Medicare prescription drug coverage.

[11] Medicare eligible individuals who are enrolled in Parts A and B of Medicare, may choose to enroll in a Medicare Advantage plan, and receive their Medicare services through the plan, if one is available in their area.

[12] Medicare is available for individuals or their spouses who have worked for at least 10 years in Medicare-covered employment and are 65 years old and a citizen or permanent resident of the United States. Individuals might also qualify for coverage if they are a younger person with a disability or with End-Stage Renal disease (permanent kidney failure requiring dialysis or transplant).

[13] These individuals are required to meet certain conditions, such as having no breaks in coverage of 63 or more days, and having

exhausted any continuation coverage required by the Consolidated Omnibus Budget Reconciliation Act of 1985 (COBRA). For more information about protections and requirements, see CRS Report RL31634, The Health Insurance Portability and Accountability Act (HIPAA) of 1996: Overview and Guidance on Frequently Asked Questions, by Hinda Chaikind, Jean Hearne, Bob Lyke, C. Stephen Redhead.

[14] "Current Trends and Future Outlook for Retiree Health Benefits, Now and in the Future, Findings from the Kaiser/Hewitt 2004 Survey on Retiree Health Benefits," The Henry Kaiser Family Foundation and Hewitt, Dec. 2004.

[15] 514 U.S. 73 (1995).

[16] 607 F. Supp. 196 (W.D.N.Y. 1984).

[17] See John C. Garner, Health Insurance Answer Book, 6th ed. (New York: Aspen, 2001).

[18] 220 F.3d 193 (3rd Cir. 2000).

[19] Satisfying the equal benefit test requires that a plan not provide lesser benefits for older participants compared to younger participants, and also that employers not require older participants to pay a greater percentage of the premium cost. Employers do not violate the act by permitting certain benefits to be provided by the government, that is, it is not necessary for an employer to provide health benefits which are otherwise provided by Medicare for certain participants.

[20] "Retiree Health Benefits Now and in the Future: Findings from the Kaiser/Hewitt 2003 Survey of Retiree Health Benefits," The Henry Kaiser Family Foundation and Hewitt, Jan. 2004.

[21] "National Survey of Employer-Sponsored Health Plans," 2003 Survey Report, Mercer.

[22] "Employer Health Benefits, 2004 Annual Survey," The Henry Kaiser Family Foundation and Health Research and Educational Trust.

[23] The underwriting cycle for health insurance is characterized by years of small increases in premiums followed by years of larger increases. At some point, increases become smaller and the cycle begins again. The cycles are in part the result of health insurance providers first lowering increases in order to remain competitive and then raising increases as profit margins drop and/or reserves are depleted.

[24] "National Survey of Employer-Sponsored Health Plans," 2003 Survey Tables, Mercer.

[25] The employer's subsidy covers "gross" costs, which includes any co-payments or coinsurance paid for by the retiree.

[26] In addition, under FAS 106, a pattern of repeatedly raising the caps would lead the company's auditors to conclude that the employer's substantive commitment is to provide retiree health benefits without a cap, thereby cancelling the expense reducing effect of the cap.

[27] Although the regulations issued by the Centers for Medicare and Medicaid Services (CMS) on the 28% subsidy appear to allow employers considerable leeway in meeting the actuarial standards, employers will have to wait and see how the regulations are actually implemented.

[28] For a more detailed description of health insurance coverage under COBRA, see CRS Report RL30626, Health Insurance Continuation Coverage under COBRA, by Heidi G. Yacker.

[29] The Trade Act of 2002 (P.L. 107-210) authorized a federal health coverage tax credit (HCTC) for certain individuals who are eligible for Trade Adjustment Assistance allowances because they have lost manufacturing jobs due to increased foreign imports or shifts in production outside the United States and for other individuals whose defined benefit pension plans were taken over by the Pension Benefit Guaranty Corporation due to financial difficulties. The refundable and advanceable credit is for 65% of what eligible taxpayers pay for qualified health insurance for themselves and their family members. For more information, see CRS report, RL32620, Health Coverage Tax Credit Authorized by the Trade Act, by Julie Stone-Axelrad and Bob Lyke.

[30] There are four types of these tax-advantaged accounts permitted under current law: Health Care Flexible Spending Accounts (HCFSA), Health Reimbursement Accounts (HRA), Archer Medical Savings Accounts (MSA) and, Health Savings Accounts (HSA). For more detailed information, see CRS Report RL32467, Health Savings Accounts, by Bob Lyke, Chris Peterson, and Neela Ranade, and CRS Report RL32656, Health Care Flexible Spending Accounts, by Chris Peterson and Bob Lyke.

[31] EBRI Issue Brief no. 271, July 2004.

[32] On May 18,2005, the Treasury Department and the IRS issued Notice 2005-42 which will allow employers to modify FSAs to extend the deadline up to 2 ½ months after the end of the plan year. Although helpful, this additional time would not add a significant amount of time to FSA spending deadlines.

[33] Employers may contribute to the FSA for their retired workers, even though the workers may not. However, few employers make these

contributions for their workers and given the decline in health insurance coverage, this is not a likely option for retired workers.

[34]   Employees who have contractual agreements with employers or arrangements with unions may have guarantees for health insurance coverage and may also limit an employer's ability to make changes to that coverage.

In: Pensions: Reform, Protection and Health Insurance ISBN: 1-59454-704-1
Editor: Leo A. Felton, pp. 81-99   © 2006 Nova Science Publishers, Inc.

Chapter 4

PENSION ISSUES CLOUD POSTAL REFORM DEBATE[*]

Nye Stevens

SUMMARY

Reform of the business model of the U.S. Postal Service (USPS) was given new momentum by the July 2003 report of a blue-ribbon presidential commission. The commission concluded that USPS faces a long-term decline in mail volume and revenues, and unless its finances are shored up, a taxpayer bailout or loss of universal service is threatened. The 108th Congress held a dozen hearings on the commission's report. Broad postal reform proposals, however, have been somewhat overshadowed by controversy over two pension funding issues left unsettled by passage of P.L. 108-18, the Postal Civil Service Retirement System Funding Reform Act of 2003.

The first issue is what to do with the "savings" to USPS from the reduction in its payments to the Civil Service Retirement Fund allowed by the law. Savings for the first three years were to be used to pay off the USPS debt to the Treasury, but for FY2006 and later years, the law provided that they be held in escrow pending further congressional action. Continuation of the escrow requirement greatly concerns mailers' organizations, because anticipated new rates will extract $18.3 billion from mail users over the next

---

[*] Excerpted from CRS Report RL32346. Updated June 27, 2005.

five years that cannot be used to deliver the mail or support the system. The Administration opposes removal of the escrow because it would add at least $3 billion annually to the budget deficit. One proposal is to use the escrow to set up a separate fund for retiree health benefits, lessening its budget impact.

The second issue concerns the provision in the 2003 act transferring from the Treasury to USPS responsibility for paying the retirement benefits earned by postal employees when they were members of the armed forces, a $27 billion obligation. USPS argues that the Treasury pays for military service credits held by employees of every other agency, and there is no connection between the USPS mission and that of the military. USPS points out that 90% of the obligation was incurred before USPS was established as an independent entity in 1971. The Administration, however, believes that USPS should pay the full cost of its employees' pensions, including those earned in military service, because the credits have pension value only by virtue of USPS having hired veterans in the first place. The Federal Employees Retirement System (FERS), to which all postal employees newly hired since 1984 belong, fully funds military retirement costs through agency contributions.

These two issues prevented postal reform legislation, reported without dissent by the House Government Reform and Senate Governmental Affairs Committees, from reaching the floor in the 108th Congress. Both bills would have removed the escrow requirement and relieved USPS of its current obligation to pay the military pension costs of its employees. They would also require USPS to begin funding its future retiree health care obligations. The House bill has been re-introduced in the 109th Congress as H.R. 22, and the Senate bill as S. 662. USPS has increased the pressure on Congress to act by setting a rate increase in motion. The increase, scheduled for early 2006, would add $3.1 billion to the nation's annual postage bill and increase the first class stamp by 2 cents. USPS said that the increase would not be necessary if Congress passed legislation to eliminate the escrow fund.

PENSION ISSUES CLOUD POSTAL REFORM DEBATE

Reform of the U.S. Postal Service (USPS) business model has become closely entwined with the congressional commitment to revisit the USPS pension funding reforms that Congress enacted in 2003. On the one hand, the prospect of a double-digit postage rate increase to cover pension-related obligations imposed by an act of the 108th Congress kept postal issues on the crowded legislative agenda in an election year. On the other hand, sharp differences between the Bush Administration and postal stakeholders over how postal pension obligations are to be handled brought to a temporary halt the postal reform effort that had gained some momentum from the report of a presidential blue-ribbon commission. The issues have once again reappeared on the agenda in the 109th Congress.

This report explains and analyzes the postal employee pension issues currently before Congress.

Background

For the past four years, USPS has been experiencing severe financial pressures stemming from a long-term decline in use of the mail for personal and, more lately, for business correspondence. Postal financial problems caused the Government Accountability Office (GAO; formerly General Accounting Office) to put USPS's transformation efforts on its High-Risk List of federal programs in April 2001, warning of the loss of universal service or a massive taxpayer bailout. The Comptroller General joined others in warning of a "death spiral" of rising rates causing further erosion in mail volume, and requiring further rate increases to cover the costs of the ever-growing delivery network. Three rate increases in 2001 and 2002 did not keep USPS from ending both of those years in the red. USPS also faced nearly $100 billion in unfunded liabilities for pensions, health benefits for retirees, and workers compensation obligations. USPS, its board of governors, mailers associations, and GAO all agreed that the Postal Reorganization Act of 1970 no longer provides a viable business model and must be reformed.[1]

Having placed USPS on its High Risk List, GAO found fault with the fact that no one had ever determined whether the $32 billion liability USPS was carrying on its books for retirement obligations of its employees who are still under the Civil Service Retirement System (CSRS) was an accurate figure.[2] GAO, along with nearly all other postal analysts, suspected that it was too low. GAO therefore asked the Office of Personnel Management (OPM) to recalculate the obligation so that the true extent of postal liabilities could be known. OPM's actuaries went back into the books to isolate Postal Service and postal employee contributions and interest earned on those contributions since 1971, when USPS became a standalone entity responsible for funding its own retirement obligations.

Thus it was welcome news when, on November 1, 2002, OPM Director Kay Coles James wrote the Postmaster General that the annual payments

USPS was making to the Civil Service Retirement and Disability Fund (CSRDF) under current law would eventually *overfund* the USPS liability for pensions to its CSRS retirees by $71 billion. A principal reason was that interest earnings of past contributions had been credited at a statutory rate of 5%, when in fact the average rate of return on the bonds held by the trust fund has been substantially higher.[3] In reviewing the OPM calculations, GAO put the potential overfunding even higher — as much as $103 billion — since under then-current law the Treasury rather than USPS was responsible for retirement benefits based on prior military service of postal employees, and OPM's calculations treated these as obligations of the Postal Service.[4]

The Postal Civil Service Retirement System Funding Reform Act of 2003

The Postal Service, its unions, mailers' organizations, OPM, the Treasury, and the Office of Management and Budget all coalesced in support of legislation, drafted originally by OPM, to change the statutory funding formula and relieve USPS of the obligation to overfund its liability. On April 23, 2003, President Bush signed into law the Postal Civil Service Retirement System Funding Reform Act of 2003, P.L. 108-18. The act authorized USPS to reduce its annual payments to the CSRDF by $3.5 billion in FY2003 and $2.7 billion in FY2004. Although the law was quickly passed without dissent in either chamber, two obstacles had to be bypassed along the way. One was the budget impact.

In reviewing OPM's draft of the legislation, the Congressional Budget Office (CBO) said that while the legislation would improve the financial position of USPS, it could increase deficits (or reduce surpluses) by as much as $41 billion in the unified federal budget over the 10-year period from FY2003 to FY2013, depending in part on what USPS did with the savings.[5] If USPS were to use the savings to hold down postage rates, this would reduce overall government receipts; the unified federal budget would be affected since mailers would pay less and the flow of funds to the CSRDF would be diminished. If, on the other hand, rates were not restrained and the "saved" money were used to pay down the $11.9 billion USPS debt to the Treasury's Federal Financing Bank, the impact on the unified federal budget would be limited to the reduction in the Bank's interest income. Partly in response to the CBO's report, the Senate (S. 380) and House (H.R. 735) bills directed USPS to use savings for FY2003 , FY2004, and FY2005 to reduce the Postal Service's debt to the Federal Financing Bank. Savings (or more accurately, postage receipts above what is needed to finance CSRS contributions at the new, actuarially determined rate) in subsequent fiscal years were to be held in escrow until otherwise provided in law. The final CBO cost estimate for the legislation projected a maximum budget cost of $7.2 billion over the FY2003-FY2013 period.[6]

The second issue was a provision included in the measure by OPM, where the first draft originated, relating to responsibility for military retirement obligations. This provision reversed a long-standing accounting practice that had required the taxpayer, rather than USPS, to pay the retirement costs associated with retirement credits earned by USPS employees in CSRS while they had been members of the armed forces. The legislative proposal would have USPS fund a portion of the military service costs for employees hired before 1972, and all military costs for employees hired after 1971 when USPS became independent. GAO estimated the cost of this provision to USPS as $27.9 billion.[7]

This provision troubled proponents of the bill. Eight Democrats summarized their objection to this provision in an "additional views" addendum to the House committee report on the bill:

> ... (W)e do not believe that requiring the Postal Service to pay the pension costs associated with military service is a good idea.... Under current law, Treasury pays the retirement costs related to the military service of employees in CSRS. H.R. 735 shifts the burden of costs related to military service of postal employees covered by CSRS to the Postal Service. In fact, the bill not only requires the Postal Service to pay military pensions for current and future retirees, but it also makes the Postal Service reimburse Treasury for costs that have already been paid. The shift will require the Postal Service to pay $27.2 billion more than it otherwise would have to pay. This is unfair to the Postal Service.[8]

Because the White House signaled that it would oppose the legislation if the military pension provision were removed, Members in the House compromised on a proposal to revisit the question later. In the words of the floor manager of the bill, Chairman Tom Davis of the Government Reform Committee,

> I think this is an issue that demands further study because no other agency in the Federal Government that I am aware of funds its

CSRS military obligations within the department. It may ultimately be unfair to make postal customers and ratepayers fund military retirement benefits. Working with the gentleman from California (Mr. Waxman), my ranking member, I prepared an amendment to the House version of the bill, H.R. 735, requiring the Department of the Treasury, the Office of Personnel Management, and the Postal Service to develop proposals on this issue. So this is an issue that will be revisited.[9]

Escrow and Military Pension Issues To Be Revisited

The military retirement issue was temporarily resolved by including in H.R. 735 a provision (Section 2 (e)) requiring USPS, the Treasury Department, and OPM each to prepare and submit to the President, Congress, and GAO, by September 30, 2003, "proposals detailing whether and to what extent the Department of the Treasury or the Postal Service should be responsible for the funding of benefits attributable to the military service of current and former employees of the Postal Service...."

With this provision added, the Senate agreed to substitute the text of S. 735 for that of S. 380, and passed the measure by voice vote on April 2, 2003.[10] Since S. 380 as passed by the Senate contained the above language approved by the House Government Reform Committee, passage of S. 380 in the House was not controversial. It passed on April 8, 2003, by a vote of 424-0.[11] President George W. Bush signed the bill into law, as P.L.108-18, on April 23, 2003.

As enacted, P.L. 108-18 clearly contemplated that both the escrow and the military retirement provisions would need to be reconsidered. In addition to the reports required of USPS, the Treasury, and OPM on the military retirement cost issue, the law also required (Section 3(e)) that USPS, by September 30, 2003, develop and submit a proposal for the use of savings that would accrue from the law's enactment after FY2005. GAO was directed to review the reports from USPS and the executive branch on military retirement costs, and, within 60 days of receiving the USPS proposal for use of the escrowed savings, to submit to Congress a written evaluation of this proposal. Section 4 of the act ("Legislative Action") provided that

Not later than 180 days after it has received both the proposal of the Postal Service and the evaluation of such proposal by the

General Accounting Office under this subsection, Congress shall revisit the question of how the savings accruing to the Postal Service as a result of the enactment of this Act should be used.

This provision, while not binding, contemplated that Congress would revisit the escrow requirement by the end of May, 2004.

Administration and USPS Proposals Differ

In the two years that has passed since enactment of P.L. 108-18, little progress has been made in resolving the issues that were left open by that legislation, despite the preparation of multiple reports and the holding of a dozen congressional hearings where the issues were discussed. The position taken by the Administration is sharply opposed to that taken by USPS and its stakeholders, and GAO's reviews of the contrasting analyses have not resolved the differences.

Proposals for Use of Escrow Funds

In its report on use of the savings in escrow after 2005, USPS pointed out that "savings" is really a misnomer for the "potential amount of overfunding of CSRS pension costs in any given year had corrective action not been enacted."[12] By the end of FY2005, USPS said that all of the overfunding in FY2003 through FY2005 will have been used to reduce debt and keep postage rates steady.[13] In the future, there will be no savings because USPS will need to build into its rates the cost of funding the escrow account, an amount that would add 5.4% (or 2 cents on a first class stamp) to whatever rate increase will otherwise be required in 2006. While it would be forced to collect the funds from the mailing public, it would not be able to use them for any purpose under the terms of P.L. 108-18. CBO estimated that the escrow requirement will cost USPS (and therefore the mailing public) nearly $3 billion in 2006 and $36 billion over the 2006-2014 time period.[14]

Nevertheless, USPS recognized that simply revoking the escrow requirement and not collecting the funds was not a realistic option, because of its negative effect on the unified federal budget. Instead, it took into account the need (emphasized by GAO and specifically identified in the statute for USPS to consider in its plan) to begin funding the liability USPS faces for the future health benefits of its retirees and their dependents, an amount it estimated at $47-57 billion. USPS proposed to devote all of the "savings" to that purpose if Congress relieved it of the burden of paying retirement benefits for military service. If Congress does not change the military service requirement, then USPS would propose to use the escrow fund amount to pre-fund retiree health benefits only for new employees, and ameliorate future rate increases by using the rest of the funds for debt repayment and capital investments. This would at least assure that postal ratepayers providing the funds would get some benefit in terms of a contribution to the costs of delivering the mail, rather than having them sit unused. USPS also expected that continuing to collect the funds but setting them aside in a fund controlled by the executive branch would neutralize the budget impact. USPS included tables in its report showing how the escrow would grow in the years after 2006, eventually peaking at $8.7 billion annually.

GAO, as required, issued a report analyzing the two USPS proposals in November, 2003.[15] GAO did not argue for retaining the escrow provision. It found that the most equitable option was the first one (setting funds aside for all pensioners), because it struck the most equitable balance between current and future ratepayers by building benefits earned by today's employees into its rate base. Leaving those costs largely unfunded, as the second option would do, was less fair to future ratepayers. GAO expressed some skepticism about using some of the funds for capital investments since it did not believe that USPS had provided Congress with a careful investment plan tied to reducing its workforce and its physical infrastructure.

Proposals for Allocating Responsibility for Military Costs

The USPS report on military pay asked Congress to reverse the provision of P.L. 108-18 requiring USPS to pay $27 billion in military retirement costs for its employees, pointing out that more than 90% of the financial obligation is the result of military service performed before the Postal Service was created.[16] Had OPM adhered to the practice of assigning costs of military service to the Treasury, USPS would not be in the situation of overfunding its CSRS obligations in the future; they would already be overfunded by $10 billion. The USPS proposal was to return the obligation to the Treasury, and to credit the $27 billion (most of it was paid out long ago to veterans of World War II and Korea) to a separate Treasury account designated as the "Postal Service Retiree Health Benefit Fund." USPS emphasized that no agency other than USPS is responsible for CSRS costs based on past military service; the Treasury pays these costs for all federal employees under CSRS.

The Treasury/OPM report on behalf of the Administration defended the requirement that USPS, rather than the Treasury, pay these costs, calling their assignment to the Treasury "an historical accident."[17] The Administration's report started from the principle that all costs attributable to employee service after the 1971 reorganization should be paid by ratepayers rather than taxpayers. The Treasury (and the taxpayer) should cover only a pro-rated share of military service for employees who retired after 1971, based on the ratio of pre-1971 civilian service to total civilian service. Postal employees qualified for pensions based on military service (like other civil service benefits) only because USPS hired them; if they had not been hired by the government, no pension costs would have been incurred. In other words, the Treasury and OPM were saying the credits should be regarded as a fringe benefit of USPS employment rather than a fringe benefit of military service. The report pointed out that FERS, which now covers most postal employees, includes the cost of military service in its dynamic funding principles, and implied that Congress would have assigned these costs to USPS in 1971 if anyone had been thinking about such issues then.

GAO's report on the military retirement issue essentially said that the issues were matters of policy for Congress to decide.[18] The GAO report did not consider the budget scoring impact of the issue. Costs assigned to the Treasury are part of the Administration's budget, while costs paid by USPS are off-budget.

Retirement Funding Issues Addressed in Hearings

Coinciding with discussion of pension funding issues was the emergence of serious debate on broader issues of postal reform in the 108th Congress. While Representative John McHugh had tried for years to gain attention to the need for reform of the failing USPS business model, legislation drafted by his House Government Reform Postal Subcommittee had never made much headway. Postal reform re-emerged as a serious issue with the July 2003 report of the President's Commission on the United States Postal Service. The commission confirmed a long-term decline in demand for postal services, and made 35 reform recommendations to stabilize USPS financing, 18 of which would require legislative action.[19]

One of the recommendations of the President's Commission was that "[r]esponsibility for funding Civil Service Retirement System pension benefits relating to the military service of Postal Service retirees should be returned to the Department of the Treasury." In its discussion of the issue, the commission said

> No other Federal agency is required to pay such costs for its retirees under CSRS. In the Commission's view, it is inappropriate to require the Postal Service, as a self-financing entity that is charged with operating as a business, to fund costs that would not be borne by any private sector corporation (costs associated with benefits earned while the retiree was employed by another employer). In addition, requiring federal agencies financed through Congressional appropriations to cover the military retirement benefits of its employees still taps resources from the same appropriate revenue source —taxpayers. Requiring a self-financing federal entity to follow suit is wholly different. It asks those who use the nation's postal system to subsidize the U.S. military every time they use the mail.[20]

Since the release of the commission's report on July 31, 2003, 13 hearings have been held by the House Government Reform or the Senate Governmental Affairs Committee, including one joint hearing on March 23, 2004. While the overall focus of the hearings was on reform proposals, most witnesses addressed the escrow and military retirement cost issues in their statements. Nearly all of the witnesses urged that these two provisions of P.L. 108-18 be repealed because of their major impact on postage rates. Senator Susan Collins, Chair of the Senate Committee on Governmental Affairs, told Treasury Secretary John Snow at the March 23 joint hearing that "two issues that united every single witness who has testified before our committee at these six previous hearings ... are a desire to see the escrow account repealed and the return of the military pension obligation to the Treasury Department.... So the administration's is a pretty lonely voice on those two issues."[21]

Legislation Introduced in the 108th Congress

Postal stakeholders recognized that the President would likely veto a freestanding bill that would add the escrow account to the deficit and return the military retirement obligation to the Treasury. Their strategy was to package military and escrow provisions in a broader postal reform measure that enacts some of the far-reaching recommendations of the President's own blue-ribbon commission.

On May 12, 2004, Representatives Tom Davis, Waxman, Danny Davis, and McHugh introduced H.R. 4341, a comprehensive postal reform measure drawn in large part from previous postal reform efforts developed by Representative McHugh. The bi-partisan bill also contained provisions repealing the escrow provision of P.L. 108-18, and returning responsibility for the military cost of postal retirees to the Treasury Department, while also requiring the Postal Service to significantly fund its retiree health benefit liability. The bill was ordered to be reported the same day by the House Committee on Government Reform by a vote of 40-0.

Senators Collins and Carper introduced S. 2468 on May 20, 2004. The bill was similar in many respects to H.R. 4341, and would also reverse the escrow and military pension provisions of P.L. 108-18.[22] S. 2468 was approved in the Senate Governmental Affairs Committee by a 17-0 vote on June 2, 2004.

Both bills faced uncertainty in the crowded end-of-session legislative calendar. In the end, neither bill was brought to the floor for a vote. One reason was that the Administration raised the level of its opposition to the legislation very late in the session.

On November 10, 2004, the Administration circulated to insiders on the Hill a plain-paper criticism of the postal reform legislation. Later referred to as a "white paper," the two-page document led with an assertion that the bills failed the test of self-financing for USPS, citing CBO's estimates of its budget impact.

> *Treatment of Military Service Obligations* — The Administration believes that the Postal Service, not ratepayers, must continue to be responsible for its pension costs connected with military service credit for postal employees under the Civil Service Retirement System (CSRS). Last year, significant pension relief was provided for USPS totaling $78 billion. The House and Senate bills would grant an additional $27 billion in relief by transferring the military service obligation to the Treasury.

> *Elimination of the Escrow Requirement* — The House and Senate provisions making funds available to the Postal Service by abolishing the existing statutory escrow requirement in 2006 must be altered so there is no adverse budget impact. The Administration supports the underlying policy of abolishing the

escrow, and has proposed a solution to eliminate the requirement in a budget neutral manner by requiring the Postal Service to use these resources to fully pre-fund current substantial unfunded liabilities for retiree health benefits.

As it became apparent that the legislation was bogged down, mailers began to question whether P.L. 108-18 was the unalloyed boon to postal commerce that it seemed to be at the time it was enacted. The escrow requirement established by the law will cost mailers $18.3 billion out of pocket over the five-year period 2006-2010, if it is not changed. According to a widely read mailers newsletter:

> While the immediate windfall from the change in the funding formula allowed the USPS to postpone the next rate increase by two years, the organization now finds itself facing the real possibility it will have to build those $3 billion costs back into the next rate case **and** absorb the military retirement costs. In short, it gets no savings in 2006 plus it has to pick up the military costs of $27 billion — a cost it didn't have to pay in the past.... (P)erhaps the industry would have been better off if the CSRS law were never changed. The question will be moot only if Congress can pass legislation lifting the escrow requirement and shifting the military costs to the Treasury.[23]

Legislative Action in the 109th Congress

Representative McHugh re-introduced the House version of postal reform legislation with only minor modifications as H.R. 22 on the first day of the 109th Congress, for himself, Government Reform Committee Chairman Tom Davis, Ranking Minority Member Waxman, and Representative Danny Davis. According to the Committee's website, "overall, the major provisions of the Postal Accountability and Reform Act remain the same as the version introduced last year."[24] H.R. 22 was reported by the House Government Reform Committee by a 39-0 vote on April 13, 2005 (H.Rept. 109-66).

The Senate bill, S. 662, was introduced on March 17, 2005 by Senators Collins, Carper, and Voinovich, and was referred to the Committee on Homeland Security and Governmental Affairs. It was ordered reported by a 15-1 vote of the Committee on June 22, 2005.

USPS increased pressure on Congress to act by announcing that it would file a 5.4% rate increase request with the Postal Rate Commission in April 2005. The Postmaster General told the National Postal Forum on March 21 that the increase —amounting to $3.1 billion and a 2-cent increase in the first class stamp beginning in January 2006 — would not be necessary if Congress would act to allow USPS to use the escrow fund for operational needs.

Analysis of Differences on the Escrow Requirement

Controversy about whether to maintain or do away with the escrow requirement imposed by P.L. 108-18 centers entirely on its budget impact. For the first three years, there was relatively little budget impact because pension costs were built into existing postage rates, and most of the proceeds were being used to retire the USPS debt to the Treasury, which is now virtually paid off.

At the March 23, 2004 joint hearing, Treasury Secretary John Snow pointed out that the escrow requirement did not originate with the Administration. He did not defend it conceptually, beyond observing that by budget scoring conventions, "if the monies are allowed to flow out of the escrow account, they would be charged against the deficit and add $3 billion to the deficit."[25] The Administration would accept an offset of this amount elsewhere in the budget, but would oppose lifting the requirement without an offset. House Government Reform Chairman Tom Davis countered that the requirement is a "job killer," because a 5.4% across the board postage increase needed to support the escrow fund would be bad for the economy. "These are postal dollars that ultimately ought to be used for the post office."[26]

The budget impact arises because if USPS were permitted to use the "savings" (or more accurately, postage receipts above what is needed to finance CSRS contributions at the current rate) for operational purposes, it would have the effect of keeping postage rates down, since it would reduce the need to charge mailers for the operational expenses covered by use of the escrow fund. A reduction in otherwise expected postage rates would reduce overall receipts to the government as measured by the unified federal budget. The problem would be solved if all of the funds were collected and transferred to the Department of the Treasury and committed to funding the Postal Service Retiree Health Benefits Fund established by the legislation; there would be no reduction in the unified federal budget. However, this would be of little benefit to mailers, because it would still keep postage rates higher than needed to support postal operations.

Both of the bills attempt to strike a balance: they would begin pre-funding the USPS obligation to pay health care costs for retirees, but at a payment level that would still allow some rate relief. Both bills would credit the retiree health care fund with the amount that P.L. 108-18 required USPS to pay for military retirement obligations. The two bills differ, however, in their payment schedules for amortizing the health care liability. S. 662 would require USPS to pay more into the retiree health benefit fund in early years but payments would be stable thereafter — a level "mortgage payments" approach. H.R. 22 requires a lower initial payment (of about 2%), but then would require sharply higher payments over the 10 subsequent years, especially from 2010 to 2015. Both bills propose a faster funding pace than USPS had proposed in its original report to Congress on the subject, but of the two, USPS prefers the level payments approach.

CBO has said that enacting H.R. 22 would not affect how much the federal government spends on pension or health care benefits for USPS retirees, but it would increase future budget deficits as measured by the unified federal budget. There would be an on-budget saving of $35.7 billion (from funding the Postal Service Retiree Health Benefits Fund in the Treasury), but an off-budget cost of $41.6 billion (nearly all from reducing postage rates), for a net cost to the unified budget of $5.9 billion for the FY2006-FY2015 period.[27]

Analysis of Differences on Military Retirement Costs

Treasury Secretary John Snow discerned that the Administration's position on the incidence of military retirement costs was not well understood by its critics in Congress and the mailing community. His statement before the March 23, 2004 joint hearing, therefore, took care to spell out in more detail the rationale behind the Administration's strong opposition to reversing the provision of P.L. 108-18 that relieved the Treasury of its obligation to pay pension costs of postal employees arising from their service in the armed forces.[28] In some contrast to the arguments made in the September 2003 OPM-Treasury report to Congress, Secretary Snow cast the argument this time in terms of general principles of equity, fairness, good government, and financial prudence.

An important element of the Administration's defense of its position is that "no other agency has ever received the benefit of a dynamic analysis of its investment flows, as was the case for the Postal Service. It provided the Postal Service with a properly calculated, enormous gain of $78 billion at the expense of other CSRS participants."[29] The statement pointed out that USPS, unlike virtually all other federal agencies, is obliged to manage its finances in a manner that covers its full costs. The Secretary also said that the Administration's proposal "is fair and equitable because the Postal Service has also been the beneficiary of significant taxpayer funded appropriations, which more than cover the attribution to Postal of the $27 billion in military costs."

The Secretary's testimony characterized the application of FERS-like principles to CSRS payments as "a 'good government' initiative."

> There are a number of voices that advocate a return of these obligations to the taxpayer because the impact on the federal budget can be minimized by having the Postal Service allocate these funds to cover other unfunded retirement obligations.... Good government dictates that we consider this as a real economic cost, dollar for dollar, no matter how these funds might be accounted for in the federal budget.[30]

Finally, the statement said it would be financially imprudent to treat USPS in a manner different from the FERS funding paradigm, because to "tinker with" FERS across agencies would have implications throughout the government retirement structure, with potentially enormous costs.

The Treasury and OPM again defended the Administration's position of military retirement obligations at an April 14, 2005 hearing of the Senate Committee on Homeland Security and Governmental Affairs. While the basic argument remained the same, some new thrusts were advanced. OPM Acting Director Dan Blair emphasized that the federal government's retirement benefit, which includes credit for military service, is a valuable component of the government's overall compensation package. USPS gains the benefits of that tool in recruitment and retention of employees, so it should pay for its full cost. In addition, he noted that Congress enacted similar pension treatment for the Patent and Trademark Office in 2004, and the President's FY2006 budget proposes continuation of the practice.

Most postal stakeholders adhere to the view that the costs of military defense should not be attributed to postal ratepayers, because they are a national obligation. While it is unlikely that USPS will be hiring many new employees who are in the CSRS system, it strikes postal stakeholders as unfair to penalize USPS for having hired veterans in the past, when USPS was required by law to give preference to veterans in hiring, and when applicants without military service credits would have been cheaper.

USPS and mailers' groups also dispute that USPS has been the beneficiary of generous appropriations from Congress. It should be noted in this regard that USPS, though entitled to by law, has not requested a public service appropriation to cover the costs of universal service since 1982, well before the advent of FERS. While USPS has received regular appropriations totaling billions as a congressional subsidy for free or reduced rate mail for non-profit organizations, the blind, and overseas voters, this was to reimburse it for not charging full costs to such beneficiaries.[31] Mailers' organizations have circulated widely a study that asserts "(i)nstead of draining the federal budget, USPS has actually been subsidizing it."[32]

While the views of USPS and mailers on the military retirement issue may be discounted because of self-interest, their position has been endorsed by at least three independent but official observers. One, as mentioned on page 8 of this report, was the President's Commission on the U.S. Postal Service. The Postal Service Office of the Inspector General (OIG) has also weighed in on the issue. The OIG issued a report saying that the decision to place additional liabilities on USPS for the escrow and military retirement costs is "wrong," and motivated by an attempt to keep higher payments coming into the CSRDF than is necessary to cover the expenses borne by postal customers. "The money should not be given to OPM to subsidize appropriated tax dollars. This would constitute a hidden tax for Postal Service customers that has not been appropriated by Congress."[33]

Finally, when asked at the April 14, 2005 Senate hearing for his views on military retirement obligations, Comptroller General David Walker responded in a way that supporters of the reform bills' approach regarded as an endorsement. He suggested that Senators use the standards of "matching" and "consistency" in evaluating the alternatives. "We should match who benefitted from the military service with the costs. I would argue that all Americans benefitted [from employees' military service]." With regard to consistency, he noted that other self-supporting organizations, including the Pension Benefit Guarantee Corporation and the Federal Deposit Insurance Corporation, do not bear responsibility for the military service costs of their employees.[34]

REFERENCES

[1] For further analysis of the causes of the long-term erosion in USPS financial prospects, see CRS Report RL31069, *Postal Service Financial Problems and Stakeholder Proposals,* by Nye Stevens. GAO has also issued a score of reports and testimonies demonstrating the point. The latest is U.S. Government Accountability Office, *U.S. Postal Service: Despite Recent Progress, Postal Reform Legislation is Still Needed,* GAO-05-453T, April 14, 2005, available at [http://www.gao.gov/new.items/d05453t.pdf].

[2] CSRS was closed to new entrants in 1984. Employees hired since then are in the Federal Employees Retirement System (FERS), a fully funded retirement system.

[3] A much more comprehensive overview of the factors involved in OPM's recalculation, including the application of dynamic principles to valuing CSRS liabilities, is contained in CRS Report RL31684, *Funding Postal Service Obligations to the Civil Service Retirement System,* by Patrick Purcell and Nye Stevens (out-of-print; available from the authors).

[4] U.S. Government Accountability Office, *Review of the Office of Personnel Management's Analysis of the United States Postal Service's Funding of Civil Service Retirement System Costs,* GAO-03-448R, Jan. 31, 2003, available at [http://www.gao.gov/new.items/d03448r.pdf].

[5] Letter to Honorable Jim Nussle, Chairman, House Budget Committee, Jan. 27, 2003, available at [http://www.cbo.gov/showdoc.cfm?index=4033&sequence=0].

[6] Congressional Budget Office, Cost Estimate, H.R. 735, Mar. 14, 2003, available at [http://www.cbo.gov/showdoc.cfm?index=4106& sequence=0].

[7] GAO 03-448R, p. 28.

[8] U.S. Congress, House Committee on Government Reform, *Postal Civil Service Retirement System Funding Reform Act of 2003,* report to accompany H.R. 735, H.Rept. 108-49, 108th Cong., 1st sess. (Washington: GPO, 2003), p. 22.

[9] Rep. Tom Davis, remarks in the House, *Congressional Record,* daily edition, vol. 149, Apr. 8, 2003, p. H2904.

[10] Senate debate, *Congressional Record,* daily edition, vol. 149, Apr. 2, 2003, pp. S4724-4729.

[11] House debate, *Congressional Record,* daily edition, vol. 149, Apr. 8, 2003, pp. H2901-2909.

[12] U.S. Postal Service, *Postal Service Proposal : Use of Savings For Fiscal Years After 2005, P.L. 108-18*, undated, available at [http://reform.house.gov/UploadedFiles/Postal%20Service%20Propos al%20-%20Use%20of%20Savings%20for%20FYs%20After%2020 05.pdf].

[13] By June 2004, USPS payments to the Treasury had reduced its debt to zero, a reduction of $11.1 billion since the end of FY2002. "Treasury Loans to USPS Fall to Zero in June Vs $7.3 Billion End FY03," *Morningstar.com*, Aug. 9, 2004.

[14] Congressional Budget Office, *Cost Estimate, H.R. 4341, Postal Accountability and Enhancement Act*, revised July 13, 2004, p. 3.

[15] U.S. Government Accountability Office, *Postal Pension Funding Reform: Issues Related to the Postal Service's Proposed Use of Pension Savings*, GAO Report GAO-04-238, Nov. 26, 2003, at [http://www.gao.gov/new.items/d04238.pdf].

[16] U.S. Postal Service, *Postal Service Proposal: Military Service Payments Requirements, P.L.. 108-18*, undated, available at [http://reform.house.gov/UploadedFiles/Postal%20Service%20Propos al%20-%20Military%20Service%20Payments%20Requirements.pdf].

[17] *Report to Congress on the Financing of Benefits Attributable to the Military Service of Current and Former Employees of the Postal Service*, undated, available at [http://www.treas.gov/press/releases/ js775.htm].

[18] U.S. Government Accountability Office, *Postal Pension Funding Reform: Review of Military Service Funding Proposals*, GAO Report GAO-04-281, Nov. 26, 2003. [http://www.gao.gov/new.items/ d04281.pdf].

[19] See CRS Report RS21640, *The Legislative Recommendations of the President's Commission on the United States Postal Service: An Overview*, by Nye Stevens and Kevin Kosar.

[20] President's Commission on the United States Postal Service, *Embracing the Future: Making the Tough Choices to Preserve Universal Mail Service: Report of the President's Commission on the United States Postal Service*, (Washington: GPO, July 31, 2003), pp. 125-126. The report is available at [http://www.treas.gov/offices/ domestic-finance/usps/].

[21] U.S. Congress, *The Postal Service in Crisis: A Joint Senate-House Hearing on Principles for Meaningful Reform*, Joint Hearing before the House Committee on Government Reform and the Senate Committee on Governmental Affairs, 108th Cong., 2nd sess, Serial No.

108-17, March 23, 2004, Washington: GPO, 2004) p. 33. (Cited hereafter as *Joint Hearing.*)

[22] For a comparison of the two bills, see CRS Report RL32402, *Postal Reform Bills: A Side-by-Side Comparison of H.R. 4341 and S. 2468*, by Kevin R. Kosar.

[23] "Benefits from CSRS Fix Are Slipping Away," *Business Mailers Review,* April 12, 2004, p. 3.

[24] [http://reform.house.gov/GovReform/News/DocumentSingle.aspx?DocumentID=6437].

[25] *Joint Hearing*, pp. 31, 33.

[26] *Joint Hearing*, p. 77.

[27] See Congressional Budget Office, *Cost Estimate, H.R. 22, Postal Accountability and Enhancement Act,* April 25, 2005, p. 1. CBO has not yet published its cost estimate for S. 662, but Chairman Collins said at the June 22, 2005 markup that the five-year cost (not the 10-year cost) had been reduced to $500 million by CBO.

[28] U.S. Department of the Treasury, *Hearing Testimony of the Honorable John W. Snow,* Mar. 23, 2004, available at [http://www.treas.gov/press/releases/ js1255.htm].

[29] Ibid., p. 2. It should be noted, however, that P.L. 108-18 made no changes in the law that raised the costs of other CSRS participants.

[30] Department of the Treasury, *Hearing Testimony,* March 23, 2004, p. 3.

[31] For more information on appropriations to USPS, see CRS Report RS21025, *The Postal Revenue Forgone Appropriation: Overview and Current Issues,* by Nye Stevens.

[32] Saturation Mailers Coalition, *The State of Pension and Retiree Benefit Obligations for the Postal Service and the Need for Reform*, Dec. 2003, available at [http://www.postcom.org/ public/2004/pension.and.benefit.pdf].

[33] U.S. Postal Service, Office of the Inspector General, *Postal Service's Funding of the Civil Service Retirement System,* product number FT-OT-04-002, April 9, 2004, p.2.

[34] U.S. Congress, Senate Committee on Homeland Security and Governmental Affairs, *U.S. Postal Service: What is Needed to Ensure its Future Viability,*109th Cong., 1st sess., April 14, 2005 (not yet published; archived Webcast available on Committee website).

INDEX